MW01698412

Building a Championship Family:

Coaching Kids' Values and Instilling Character

Building a Championship Family:

Coaching Kids' Values and Instilling Character

Gary P. Dehrer, M.Ed.

NEW HORIZON PRESS
Far Hills, NJ

New Horizon Press
P.O. Box 669
Far Hills, NJ 07931

Gary Dehrer
Building a Championship Family:
Coaching Kids' Values and Instilling Character

Cover Design: Robert Aulicino
Interior Design: Susan Ramundo

Library of Congress Control Number: 2007923140

ISBN 13: 978-0-88282-299-0
ISBN 10: 0-88282-299-3

Manufactured in the U.S.A.

2011 2010 2009 2008 2007 / 5 4 3 2 1

Dedication

For Kaye, Nancy,
Janet and Stephen

Table of Contents

MESSAGE to PARENTS

THE PARENTING CHALLENGE

Parenting is a tough and demanding job

Parenting is the raising of children, while a family is the social group that consists of parents and their offspring.

Both families and parenting have been an integral part of history through the generations. A fundamental lesson learned is that parenting done well is a tough and demanding job.

Parents must care for, feed, clothe, support, protect, train, educate and love their children. Parenting is an uncertain and adventurous journey. Many things cannot be predicted about raising children. Every day with children is an uncharted and interesting experience. Parents learn that they are *on call* twenty-four hours a day, seven days a week! The experience can range from incredible joy and satisfaction to sacrifice, worry and frustration.

Parenting in America today is facing a rising curve of expectations. Families are facing a series of formidable challenges in a world that is increasingly fast-paced, changing, indifferent, insensitive, demanding, dangerous and sometimes just plain unfair. Yet parents are expected to achieve great success with their children enabling them to be good family members, lifelong learners, good communicators, productive workers and participating citizens. Not only do parents have to rear their children, but they also have to earn a living. Facing the demands of both home and work require parents to work twice as hard at achieving success.

It has become even more difficult to raise children with two working parents. Time spent at work in pursuit of dollars takes time and energy away from the family. Parents putting their kids in day care and arriving home after a full workday have seemingly little left for family activities. The vision of a family all present for a quiet dinner and evening together has become fractured with disjointed work and lifestyles.

Traditional family support structures of interconnected neighborhoods and extended families embracing multiple generations have weakened. Increasingly, families are finding themselves more isolated and at risk of not achieving the success they should have. The rising divorce rate is further eroding the strength of the family. Parenting skills vary greatly with both positive and negative results.

FEARS AND HOPES OF PARENTS

Parents fear failure but hope for the best

It is surprising how many parents have self-doubts about their abilities to be really good parents.

In *Parenting Isn't for Cowards*, by Dr. James Dobson, parents reported self-doubts about themselves:
- "I've failed my children."
- "I'm overwhelmed by the responsibility of it all."

Dr. Dobson comments, "Isn't it incredible to observe just how tentative we have become about this task of raising children? Parenting is hardly a new technology. Since Adam and Eve graced the Garden, seventy-seven billion people have lived on this earth, yet we're still nervous about bringing up a baby. It is a sign of the times."

Within all parents lies the hope that they can, despite any barriers, become successful parents. No matter what situation or circumstance a parent is in, that hope is there. Wishing the best for your child is common but courageous actions are required to bring this wish to reality.

MEETING THE PARENTING CHALLENGE

How can parents, single parents, stepparents, adoptive parents, partners or even grandparents raising young children do a good job?

Many parents are reluctant to self-examine themselves to determine where they are with respect to parenting skills and family success.

In *Family First*, by Dr. Phil McGraw, parents are asked some tough "self-examination" questions:

- "Are you creating a family environment that brings out the best in your child?"
- "Do you have a plan and an objective in mind for what successful parenting is and will yield in your child's life?"

Dr. Phil says, "I know you have just answered these questions, but I ask you to go back and read them over again, and this time answer them keeping in mind that you are writing your children's future with your answers. Those questions are just the beginning of the self-examination you must be willing to do if you're going to strengthen the foundation on which your children are basing their lives."

A good parent has to look at themselves in the mirror and ask some tough questions. Facing reality helps to measure just how far a parent will go to make that critical difference in the life of a young child. The reality is that when you are a parent, you have the responsibility to be there for that child.

FAMILY VALUES

What values should parents teach their children?

There is no single list of values that has been universally adopted for parents.

It is important to adopt and follow a group of values that will produce positive behaviors and results. Parents need to be mindful of what specific values they want their children to learn and have a plan to model and teach them.

Any worthy and ethical set of values faithfully pursued can yield positive outcomes. While there is no single magic list of family values, the values taught in this book offer a balance and focus that can assist families in their quest for winning seasons. Values are only as strong as the effort put behind them.

TAKE THE CHAMPIONSHIP FAMILY SHORT QUIZ

Three critical questions and three responsive answers

Consider answers for these questions:

1. What VALUES should I teach my children?

2. How can I build a CHAMPIONSHIP FAMILY?

3. What can I do to sustain and reinforce a CHAMPIONSHIP FAMILY?

While answers can vary, this book advances the following responses with the hope and promise that their full implementation will sharpen the focus of your parenting skills.

The answers are:

1. There are twenty-four fundamental **Core and Life Skill Values** that can guide you and your children through every day.

2. You can follow the **Character Parenting Game Plan**.

3. You can sustain a Championship Family by reviewing the Game Plan and reinforce it by continuing the **Family Journal** project.

Three basic elements will lead to the realization of a CHAMPIONSHIP FAMILY: Core and Life Skill Values, Character Parenting Game Plan and Family Journal.

WHAT ARE THE CORE AND LIFE SKILL VALUES?

12 Core and 12 Life Skill Values form the Championship Family framework

The **Core Values** consist of ABILITY, CHARACTER, RESPECT, CARING, FAITH, LOVE, MORAL COURAGE, TRUTH, RESPONSIBILITY, SERVICE, TACT and VIRTUE.

The **Life Skill Values** consist of MOTIVATION, PERSEVERANCE, CREATIVITY, FITNESS, COMMUNICATION, CONFIDENCE, JUDGMENT, KNOWLEDGE, DECISION MAKING, LEADERSHIP, ORGANIZATION and TEAMWORK.

HOW DOES THE CHARACTER PARENTING GAME PLAN WORK?

Parents take their children to a TRAINING CAMP to start the process

The road to becoming a Championship Family starts with the Character Parenting Game Plan by sending your family to a special training camp.

The first value that you will encounter is ABILITY, with your kids learning that they are uniquely special and talented. Children will understand how important it is to be the person they were meant to be and to identify their own "footprints in the sand." More lessons and activities follow as parents coach their kids through twenty-three more values and more.

This book offers parents a powerful tool in helping to guide their elementary age children in having the best possible chance at capturing some great values that will accompany them for the rest of their lives.

Character Parenting is:

- Making a substantial investment (you and your resources) in your children's life.
- Spending quality time with your children.
- Giving your children the gift of good character.
- Being there as your children's first and most important coach and teacher.
- Empowering your children with a winning value system.

PARENTS AS CHARACTER COACHES

Yes, you blow the whistle and carry the clipboard!

Now you are ready to build your own CHAMPIONSHIP FAMILY using the lessons, activities and resources of this book.

Parents, as coaches, must be ready and willing to blow the whistle and mark their clipboards as their children go through their character value training.

You must be willing to spend quality time with your children.

Quality time varies, from having a meal together, watching a movie together, playing a game of catch, or having a one-on-one conversation. Quality time is whenever parents and children are focused on one another exclusively.

> Parents, be there for your children as their character coach and your family will forever have Championship Seasons.
>
> *Coaching Tip*

Character is one of the most important qualities a person can have.

Your faithful dedication as a character coach will affirm, strengthen, or change the course and direction of your family. Parents coaching their children in developing character will transform a family into an unbeatable team where everyone can:

- **Soar** to their dreams.
- **Imagine** impossible things.
- **Pursue** goals with persistence.
- **Create** unbelievable things.
- **Thrive** for a lifetime!

MESSAGE to KIDS

On Being a Champion

During his short life, Matthew 'Mattie' Stepanek accomplished some exceptional things. At the age of three, Mattie started saying poetry, which his mother wrote down for him. At the age of four Mattie started saying the word "heartsong," which he would later define as "your inner beauty, the song in your heart that wants you to help make yourself a better person, and to help other people do the same. Everybody has one." At the age of ten, Mattie was very ill battling a rare form of muscular dystrophy that he had suffered from since birth. Doctors were certain Mattie was dying and asked him if he had a final wish. Mattie responded with three wishes:

- To publish a book of his poetry.
- To appear on Oprah Winfrey's television show.
- To meet his hero, former President Jimmy Carter.

Remarkably, Mattie would get all three wishes and survive another three years before dying at the age of thirteen in 2004. Writing nearly 2,000 poems, Mattie would publish five books of poetry selling more than 1.5 million copies by 2004. Appearing on "*Oprah*," Mattie became a favorite guest and was named the Muscular Dystrophy Association's goodwill ambassador. After the terrorist attack on the New York World Trade Center on September 11, 2001, Mattie wanted to work and be known as a peacemaker. After meeting Mattie, Jimmy Carter said, "Mattie was something special, something very special."
Mattie Stepanek's philosophy of life was:

- Play after every storm.
- Celebrate life every day in some way.
- If you want something bad enough, never give up and you will succeed.

Mattie experienced plenty of storms in his life. Despite living with an illness that impairs breathing, digestion, and heart rate, Mattie played, celebrated, and never gave up. Mattie said, "We all have life storms, and when we get through them or recover from them, we should celebrate that we got through it. That's what my life's philosophy means: to remember to play after every storm."

This book is about good values, interacting, building relationships, developing family traditions, and creating championship families with character and values.

This book is very much about being a *champion—playing, celebrating, and never giving up . . . and letting your heart sing.*

CHARACTER PARENTING

Parents teach their children lessons and coach activities in character values

CHARACTER PARENTING involves lessons and activities for twenty four positive and moral values to help children gain experience and build habits of good character. Consisting of twelve Core and twelve Life Skill values, they constitute character fundamentals.

CHARACTER PARENTING provides character instruction for your children, thereby creating a Championship Family. Character coaching serves as the process and the family championship seasons are the outcome.

CHARACTER PARENTING offers parents many options to teach/ coach character values. Good character is achieved through making positive choices and forming good habits. Parents need to model good character for their children. Parents need to provide their time in teaching their children character values which strengthen family relationships and promote lifestyles centered around great values.

A family with character is a championship family

PARENTS MAKE THE DIFFERENCE

Good parenting is intertwined with family character training

The lessons, activities and journals in this book are aimed at young children in their elementary school age years. CHARACTER PARENTING can make a difference with young children in their formative years before any bad habits may develop and routines become too ingrained. However, it is never too late for anyone to work on character improvement! The good character exhibited by a family is the report card of good parenting.

Parents have the responsibility of providing the best possible guidance and support. Good parenting skills rest not only on the love a parent can give their child, but also on the implementation of adequate character training and modeling. **Good character is one of the greatest traits a parent can give their children.**

> Parents must be proactive in providing lessons in character for their children that are value driven. Character Parenting must start as early as possible in the life of a family and never stop.
>
> *Coaching Tip*

The **CHARACTER PARENTING GAME PLAN** focuses on character fundamentals that include twenty-four positive moral values, each with a separate lesson and activity.

Lessons—These teach fundamental Core and Life Skill Values that help expand scope of character. The values provide a basic framework for character development and need to be emphasized in the home first.

- Lessons form the theory of Character Parenting.
- Lesson are the workout sessions.
- Lessons are the "guided practice" sessions for families.
- Lessons learned provide the foundation of Character Parenting.

Activities—This aids parents and their children in exploring and applying character values together. These activities address opportunities for character growth and need to be completed as joint parent and child enterprises.

- Activities are the practice of Character Parenting.
- Activities are the hands-on experiences.
- Activities open the way for "independent practice" sessions for families.
- Activities completed provide the building on top of the foundation.

Interaction and communication between parents and their children is the heart of the **CHARACTER PARENTING GAME PLAN**. Mutual involvement in the lessons and activities, as well as the journal exercises, will produce both immediate and long range results in the building of character values within the family.

CHARACTER PARENTING GAME PLAN

I. **TRAINING CAMP**—Starting and continuing with five basic values

ABILITY*—LIFE FOOTPRINTS
CHARACTER*—CHARACTER TOWER
MOTIVATION—SHOOTING STARS
PERSEVERANCE—FAMILY ACTION PLAN
RESPECT*—FRIENDSHIP CHECKLIST

II. **CONDITIONING**—Building the inner strength to live a life of character

CARING*—THANK YOU CARDS
CREATIVITY—NEW INVENTION
FAITH*—BIBLE CUBE
FITNESS—4-WEEK CHALLENGE
LOVE*—FAMILY TRADITIONS
MORAL COURAGE*—PROFILE IN COURAGE
TRUTH*—FIVE QUESTIONS

III. **PRACTICE SESSIONS**—Acquiring the habits of good character

COMMUNICATION—FAMILY NEWSLETTER
CONFIDENCE—RESUME
JUDGMENT—FIVE TESTS
KNOWLEDGE—FAMILY OF READERS
RESPONSIBILITY*—NO EXCUSES

IV. **GAME TIME**—Demonstrating the power of good character

DECISION MAKING—SEVEN STEPS
LEADERSHIP—GREATEST PRESIDENTS
ORGANIZATION—CLUTTER FREE
SERVICE*—SERVICE ABOVE SELF
TACT*—DIPLOMACY GAME
TEAMWORK—DESIGN CITY
VIRTUE*—MORAL COMPASS

V. **CHAMPIONSHIP SEASONS**—Sustaining great character for a lifetime

SOAR

IMAGINE

PURSUE

CREATE

THRIVE

***Core Values**; unmarked ones are **Life Skill Values**

FAMILY JOURNAL

FAMILY JOURNAL is a collaborative writing and scrapbook project involving the entire family. Every member has the opportunity to work on the journal and it should reflect the participation and contributions of everyone, including grandparents and extended family. Make liberal and frequent use of family photos. Above all else, the journal activities should be fun!

The FAMILY JOURNAL sections include:

JOURNAL: INTRODUCTIONS

- **FAMILY JOURNAL** (Title Page/Family Photograph)
- **FAMILY COAT of ARMS and MOTTO**
- **FAMILY MEMBER INTRODUCTIONS**

JOURNAL: LIFESTYLE

- **FAMILY HOBBIES**
- **FAMILY SPORTS**
- **FAMILY COOKBOOK**
- **FAMILY HUMOR**
- **FAMILY BEST TIMES**

JOURNAL: GREATEST STORIES

- **FAMILY STORYTELLING**
- **FAMILY SHORT STORIES**
- **FAMILY HISTORY**

JOURNAL: CELEBRATIONS!

- **FAMILY BIRTHDAYS**
- **FAMILY AWARDS and ACHIEVEMENT**
- **FAMILY WEDDINGS**
- **FAMILY VICTORIES and OTHER SPECIAL DAYS**
- **FAMILY ART and POETRY**

With a total of 168 hours available in every week (seven days, twenty-four hours), Championship Family parents should be able to spend more than the reported national average of seven minutes per week of dedicated one-on-one time with their children.

Each section of the Family Journal will prompt family members to contribute and make it a family enterprise. One of the first journal assignments calls for everyone to write their own introductions of themselves giving some personal background information and listing their current interests and future goals/plans. The journal project is an extension of the lessons and activities that are included in this book.

Get ready to have some fun together. Get ready for some meaningful interaction. Get ready to do a Championship Family Journal!

CHAPTER ONE

TRAINING CAMP: (Basics)

Your children's trip to TRAINING CAMP begins as soon as they are brought into this world. From the day they are born, your unconditional love and total support began to get them ready for life. Championship Families start their winning seasons by rigorous training and practice in the basic fundamentals of ABILITY, CHARACTER, MOTIVATION, PERSEVERANCE and RESPECT. Winning comes from realizing and practicing these fundamentals. TRAINING CAMP is where parents and children:

- Start with the five **VALUES.**
- Recognize and appreciate their own special **ABILITIES.**
- Develop and build habits of **CHARACTER.**
- Learn to be alive and active through **MOTIVATION.**
- Unleash the sheer power and force of **PERSEVERANCE.**
- Understand the wisdom of **RESPECT.**

Parents, take your children to TRAINING CAMP with high expectations. Their footprints in the sand and shaping of values, conscience, and courage are set in motion opening the way to a life of satisfaction and happiness. Coach and teach them well so they can be the person they were meant to be, always have the courage to do the right thing, light their fire, be considerate and never give up!

Coaching Tip

1. Lesson on **ABILITY**

> Spending quality time with your children, helping them to know themselves and their special abilities are critically important.
>
> ***Coaching Tip***

ABILITY Lesson Objectives:

- Children will write a definition of ABILITY.
- Parents will give their children positive verbal reinforcement.

Parents should:

1. Discuss a short definition of ABILITY. A parents' belief in their children's abilities should never waiver, regardless of any handicaps or disabilities. Children's abilities can take many different forms, and these skills can unfold at any time. Everyone should be the person they were meant to be, and this involves identifying and developing abilities. Several identified abilities and talents of your child should be part of their definition of ABILITY.

2. Parent to Child Dialogue (positive verbal reinforcement):

✓ "You are a very special person."

✓ "You have learned to do that very well."

✓ "Good job!"

✓ "Let's put your drawing up on the wall!"

✓ "You have a real talent for that."

✓ "Let's save all the good examples of your work in a binder."

✓ "I am proud of you and all the things you can do!"

3. Discuss how a person's abilities play a vital role in how they live life. The footprints all of us leave in life should reflect the best of our abilities and talents. Abilities are valuable resources and children need to become very familiar with all that they have.

> Imagine that your children will accomplish great and noble deeds, never stop encouraging such outcomes.
>
> *Coaching Tip*

ABILITY

It all begins with your ability to do something; to accomplish a wide range of physical and mental tasks. An individual's capacity to perform various endeavors is at the heart of fulfilling their role as a family member, citizen, worker and lifelong learner. Abilities stem from natural talents and acquired skills. Everyone has certain aptitudes that are waiting to be discovered and developed. Your competence as a person is based on your ability to perform daily activities with some degree of confidence and success. Work to develop the abilities—talents and skills of all family members.

The key to unlocking and realizing individual abilities is making the determined effort to identify, use and enhance them. Of course this involves work—hard work at times but the effort is more than worth the hassle and stress. Talent is a wonderful gift, but if it is not worked on and developed to its fullest measure, then it is wasted. Skills can be learned and perfected and this is why everyone can display ability in their life and gain the satisfaction of accomplishment and achievement.

❖ **Never doubt that you have the ABILITY to handle problems and to successfully cope with the challenges of life; develop your children's talents and skills to their greatest extent!**

ABILITY—"A Psalm of Life"
Henry Wadsworth Longfellow
Lesson 125, *McGuffey's Sixth Eclectic Reader*

A PSALM OF LIFE
"Lives of great men all remind us
We can make our lives sublime,
And, departing, leave behind us
Foot-prints on the sands of time"

ABILITY—Questions:
1. What is Longfellow telling us?

2. Are you living your life actively and meaningfully?

3. What *footprints* are you leaving on the *sands of time?*

4. What are you doing to develop your skills and talents to their fullest measure?

5. Where do you see your abilities taking you?

LIFE FOOTPRINTS ACTIVITY

Never miss an opportunity to tell your children that they have unique abilities and talents. Always tell your children that you believe in them.

Coaching Tip

Children should:
- Develop a "footprint" list of some of the major things they have learned, accomplished and would like to achieve in the years to come.
- Answer the question: "What great thing do I want to accomplish with my life?"
- Using my template, make a pathway of footprints with those things learned, accomplished and future achievements.

❖ **ASSIGNMENT: Help your children to identify their "footprints" and make a "pathway" to display them.**

1. **Parents will help their children develop their "footprint" list of the major things they have learned, accomplished and would like to achieve with their lives.** It is amazing what children have learned at home, in the community and at school. Everything should be considered from intellectual to physical skills and activities. Things accomplished can include both minor and major items. Sometimes a seemingly small success can lead to a more significant one. Future achievements really have no limitations. Consider all of the hopes and dreams that can be imagined for your child.

2. **In answering the question, "What great thing do I want to accomplish with my life?" children need to focus on one major life goal.** A child could single out a future career or single out a great accomplishment. In answering this question, the reason for the choice also needs to be explained. The *why* behind the goal needs to be discussed along with steps that need to be taken to reach your life's goal.

When a child knows that a parent believes in him or her, and can feel their unconditional approval, great things happen. Parental support of their children sets in motion an unbelievable chain of events resulting in kids reaching their highest levels of accomplishment and achievement. It is amazing what a little praise and encouragement can do in the life of anyone, especially for a child to receive some words of encouragement from a parent.

A little encouragement = incredible accomplishments!

3. **Parents will assist their children in putting together a pathway of footprints**. Remember, this pathway could go all around a child's room and even lead around the house. Our life's footprints are without boundaries.

- Using the footprint template make several dozen copies on different colored construction paper.
- Write an item on each footprint from your prepared list.
- Put up your pathway of footprints and let it run up the wall, over the ceiling and even out the door down the hall!
- Let your children's imagination and creativity push past their normal limits. This is a practice that needs to be repeated often with other activities and throughout life.

> Make supreme sacrifices for your children; pay any price and bear any burden for them.
>
> *Coaching Tip*

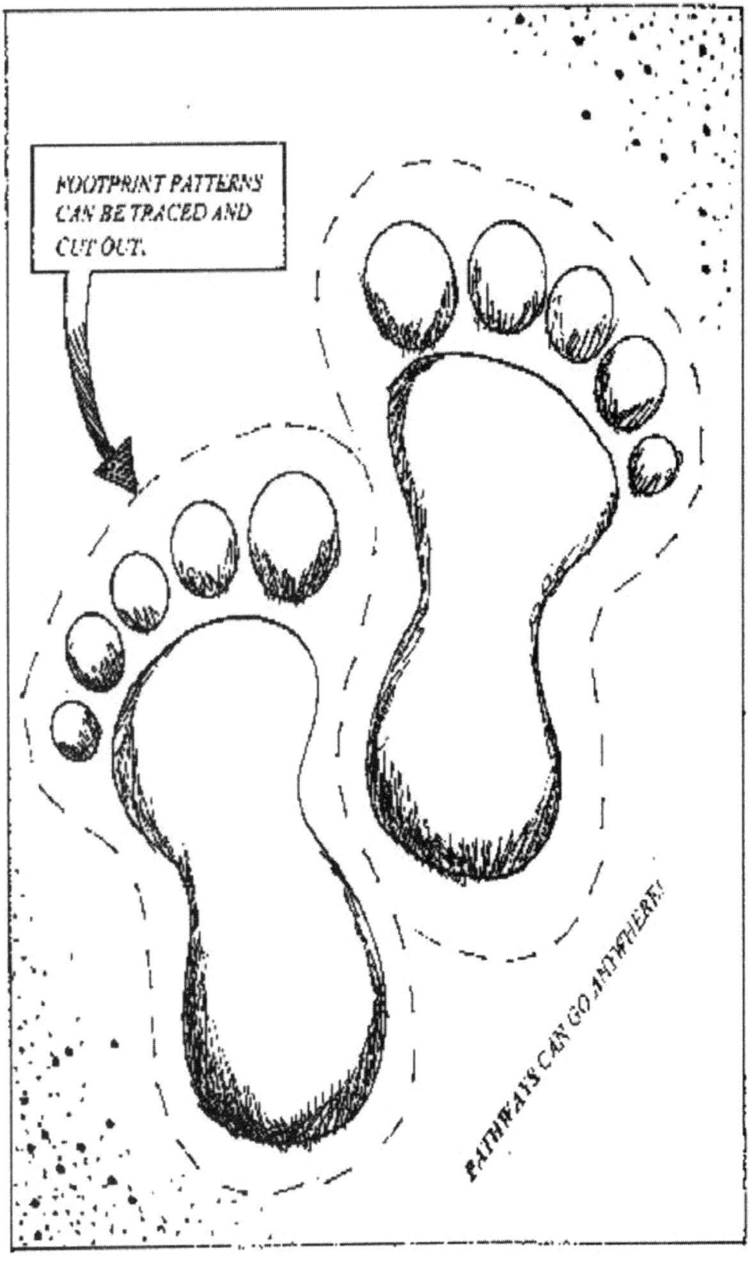
FOOTPRINT PATTERNS CAN BE TRACED AND CUT OUT.
PATHWAYS CAN GO ANYWHERE!

2. Lesson on **CHARACTER**

> Good character exceeds any other personal achievement.
>
> *Coaching Tip*

CHARACTER Lesson Objectives:
- Children will write a definition of CHARACTER
- Parents will give their children positive verbal reinforcement.

Parents should:
1. Read the introductory summary on CHARACTER and discuss a concise definition that includes its three basic components: values, conscience and courage. The CHARACTER of a person reflects their positive thoughts and actions. Prompts and other assistance from parents may be needed to help children write their definition. Good character is simply the best any of us can be, and this thought should be in your child's definition.

2. Parent to Child Dialogue (positive verbal reinforcement):

✓ "I'm proud that you did the right thing."

✓ "By standing up for what was right, you showed great courage."

✓ "You are a good person."

✓ "I admire what you did."

✓ "Thank you for being such a responsible person."

✓ "You knew what was right and then went ahead and did it!"

✓ "You are to be commended for your actions."

The DECLARATION OF INDEPENDENCE can be divided into four parts:

- The Preamble
- A Declaration of Rights
- A Bill of Indictment
- A Statement of Independence

*Look up underlined words with your children in a dictionary.

CHARACTER

How would someone who knows you describe the kind of person you are? Do you think that their description would match the perception you have of yourself? Your character is really what people would be describing, and that description contains those qualities and features that set you apart. An important part of a person's attributes, traits and abilities is their moral and ethical makeup which gives their character its true nature and meaning. Your goodness brightens your character and gives it sparkle and depth. Character parenting is centered on developing and strengthening good character traits in children. The Championship Family is built around strongly held character values.

The character of a person truly casts a giant shadow revealing who they really are. Character is your leading edge in meeting others at every turn throughout the days of your life. It makes sense that this "leading edge" should reveal you at your very best in terms of moral and ethical values. Your character should reflect your own "empire of values."

❖ **Your character is the sum total of the *values* you hold, your *conscience* about right conduct and your *courage* to act ethically; good character literally towers over academic, work, athletic or artistic accomplishments.**

CHARACTER—DECLARATION OF INDEPENDENCE (1776)
Thomas Jefferson

Preamble to the DECLARATION OF INDEPENDENCE

"When in the Course of human events, it becomes necessary for one people to dissolve the political bands which have connected them with another, and to assume among the powers of the earth, the separate and equal station to which the Laws of Nature and of Nature's God entitle them, a decent respect to the opinions of mankind requires that they should declare the causes which impel them to the separation."

The Declaration continues with . . .
"We hold these truths to be self-evident, that all Men are created equal, that they are endowed by their Creator with certain inalienable Rights, that among these are Life, Liberty and the pursuit of Happiness—"

CHARACTER—Questions:

1. Who was George Washington?

2. Who was Thomas Jefferson?

3. Who was Benjamin Franklin?

4. What is a preamble?

5. What was the purpose of the Declaration of Independence?

CHARACTER TOWER ACTIVITY

> Tell your children that their character is held up by the strong pillars of trustworthiness, respect, responsibility, fairness, caring, and citizenship.
>
> *Coaching Tip*

Children should:

- List and briefly describe the Six Pillars of Character.
- Give an example of how they can demonstrate each of the six character ethical values.
- Construct a "Character Tower" with captions and quotes.

❖ **ASSIGNMENT: Teach your children about the Six Pillars of Character and help them construct a "Character Tower."**

1. **Parents will examine the Six Pillars of Character with their children.** Parents should first read through the six core values with their children. Each value will be discussed and then children will be asked to recite the six values from memory. These values need to be memorized as they are essential to showing good character. These are the "pillars" that children need to sustain in their daily activities. Values are a foundation for families with character.

2. **Children should give an example of how they can show each of the six character ethical values.**

☐ Why is being truthful sometimes difficult?

☐ How do you keep yourself from becoming angry and using bad language?

☐ What have you done recently to show you are responsible?

☐ How are you fair to others?

☐ How do you help others?

☐ What can you do to make the community a better place to live?

3. **Construct a "Character Tower" using pillar captions and milk cartons.** The tower symbolizes how you will act as a person while your life footprints show where you are going with your life. A person's good character reaches up high while displaying ethical values.

☐ Use the pillar design shown in the CHARACTER PILLARS Activity graphic as a guide for this. Parents will help their children make about two dozen paper pillars approximately eight inches tall. On each pillar write one of the character ethical values or a quote that illustrates what these values are all about. A reference book on quotations can be used or quotes can be made up by you and your children.

☐ Once the pillars are done, place them on fifteen empty one quart milk cartons. Refer to activity graphic showing a Character Tower. Note that some of the cartons will have one pillar glued on while the corner cartons will need two pillars. Five of the cartons used for support will not have any pillars.

☐ Actual tower design can vary, stand free, or be up against a wall. There is no set design for individual character.

☐ Assembled tower can be displayed anywhere in the house. *Character Tower could be placed near the start of your child's Ability Footprints Pathway.*

A good reference for displaying exemplary character would be the "Six Pillars of Character," created by Michael Josephson of The Josephson Institute. These six pillars consist of trustworthiness, respect, responsibility, fairness, caring and citizenship. For more information, visit the Josephson Institute.

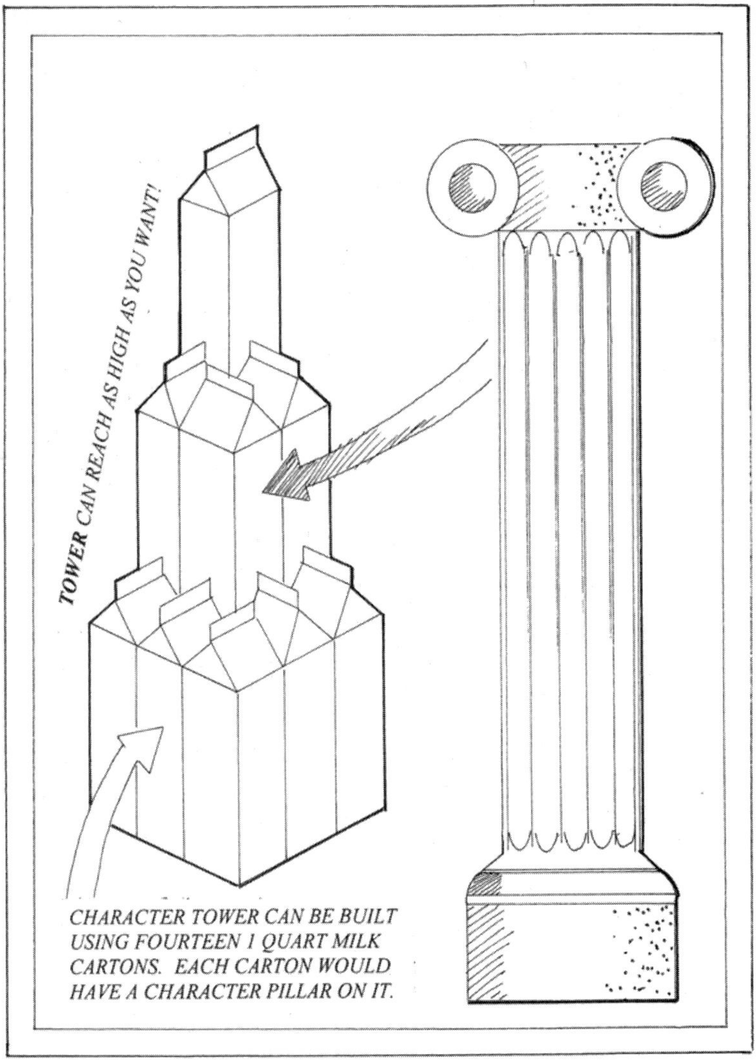
TOWER CAN REACH AS HIGH AS YOU WANT!
CHARACTER TOWER CAN BE BUILT USING FOURTEEN 1 QUART MILK CARTONS. EACH CARTON WOULD HAVE A CHARACTER PILLAR ON IT.

3. Lesson on **MOTIVATION**

> The hardest part of any job is getting started. Use *motivation* as your principal self-starter.
>
> ***Coaching Tip***

MOTIVATION Lesson Objectives:
- Children should write a definition of MOTIVATION.
- Parents will give their children positive verbal reinforcement.

Parents should:
1. Read the introductory summary on MOTIVATION and discuss a short definition of this powerful value. Definition should include some reference to the twin powers of enthusiasm and passion. These are two qualities that produce fire in motivation.

2. Parent to Children Dialogue (positive verbal reinforcement):

✓ "Yes, you've got a great idea!"

✓ "This is a wonderful start, now keep going!"

✓ "Talk about how it can be done, not how it can't."

✓ "Always be enthusiastic in life."

✓ "It is good that you have so many interests."

✓ "Anything you love to do, you will do very well."

✓ "Motivation leads to excellence in what you do."

The Cold War waged from 1945 to 1989. America triumphed as the Soviet Union collapsed under the weight of serious economic difficulties and Russia ended its communist period. The most dangerous point in the Cold War was in 1962 with the Cuban Missile Crisis when the United States directly confronted the Soviet Union. Confrontation had resulted from the placing of Russian missiles and nuclear warheads in Cuba threatening the security of the United States. President Kennedy ordered a naval blockade of Cuba and prepared for the invasion of Cuba if necessary. The Soviet Union backed down and removed its weapons from Cuba, thus averting any further escalation.

MOTIVATION

Motivation has two basic components that make it the driving and sustaining force that it is: enthusiasm and passion. To be enthusiastic is to be excited about life and its unlimited possibilities! Enthusiastic people are interested in everyone and everything around them and their vitality is pervasive. The powerful emotion of passion is the building block of love and joy. Passionate people are filled with stimulation and energy; they are on the move. Motivated people are the movers and shakers of the world; they make things happen.

Intelligence and talent are stagnated without the impulse and activity of motivation. Apathy is hiding from life and yourself. You must wholeheartedly engage in the act and process of being motivated. Parents need to constantly model motivation for their children. Your skills and abilities will thrive through motivation. There is no excuse for not being the most enthusiastic and passionate person you know!

❖ **Be enthusiastic and motivated about life, be constantly amazed and curious about the world around you. Otherwise, you risk mediocrity or worse.**

LIGHT YOUR FIRE!

Help your children to become *positive* and *enthusiastic* people filled with curiosity and many interests.

Coaching Tip

MOTIVATION—INAUGURAL ADDRESS of JOHN F. KENNEDY - January 20, 1961 (Excerpt from Speech)

We dare not forget today that we are heirs of the first revolution. Let the word go forth from this time and place, to friend and foe alike, that the torch has been passed to a new generation of Americans—born in this century, tempered by war, disciplined by a hard and bitter peace, proud of our ancient heritage—and unwilling to witness or permit the slow undoing of those human rights to which this nation has always been committed, and to which we are committed today at home and around the world.

Let every nation know, whether it wishes us well or ill, that we shall pay any price, bear any burden, meet any hardship, support any friend, oppose any foe, in order to assure the survival and success of liberty.

To those old allies whose culture and spiritual origins we share, we pledge the loyalty of faithful friends. United, there is little we cannot do in a host of cooperative ventures. Divided, there is little we can do—for we dare not meet a powerful challenge at odds and split asunder.

And so, my fellow Americans, ask not what your country can do for you; ask what you can do for your country.

My fellow citizens of the world: Ask not what America will do for you, but what together we can do for the freedom of man.

MOTIVATION—Questions:

1. Who was John F. Kennedy?

2. How does President Kennedy motivate Americans at the end of his speech?

3. What passages from this speech do you consider especially motivational? Why?

4. When President Kennedy said, "Ask not what your country can do for you; ask what you can do for your country," what was he saying?

5. Consider another version of the above quote, "Ask not what your family can do for you; ask what your can do for your family." What does this mean to you?

SHOOTING STARS Activity

> What your children feel in a moment of inspiration can forever change the course and direction of their lives.
>
> ***Coaching Tip***

Children should:

- Select inspirational quotes from John F. Kennedy's Inaugural Address.
- Find and write additional inspirational quotes.
- Create a "galaxy" of shooting stars ready for display.

❖ **ASSIGNMENT: Discuss inspirational quotes with your children and help them create a "galaxy" of shooting stars.**

1. Parents will help their child find additional inspirational and motivational quotes. Some of these can be originally created by parents and children. Quotation reference books can easily be found in bookstores, libraries and even online. A good quote is measured by its depth of meaning and economy of words. Whenever someone else's quote is written down, always indicate who wrote it. Children should be taught to never take credit for someone else's work. Quotation marks indicate that the authorship of a written passage is the work of another person. You will need a quote for each of the fifty shooting stars that will be completed.

2. Using the "Shooting Stars" guide construct fifty stars. These stars can be cut out of construction paper. If white paper is used, color each star with a different color. The edges of the stars could also be decorated with designs. Write a quotation on each star. Once the stars have been completed, display them on a wall, ceiling, or door. Your children's galaxy of stars will help to serve as a motivational reminder that so much can be accomplished with the right attitude.

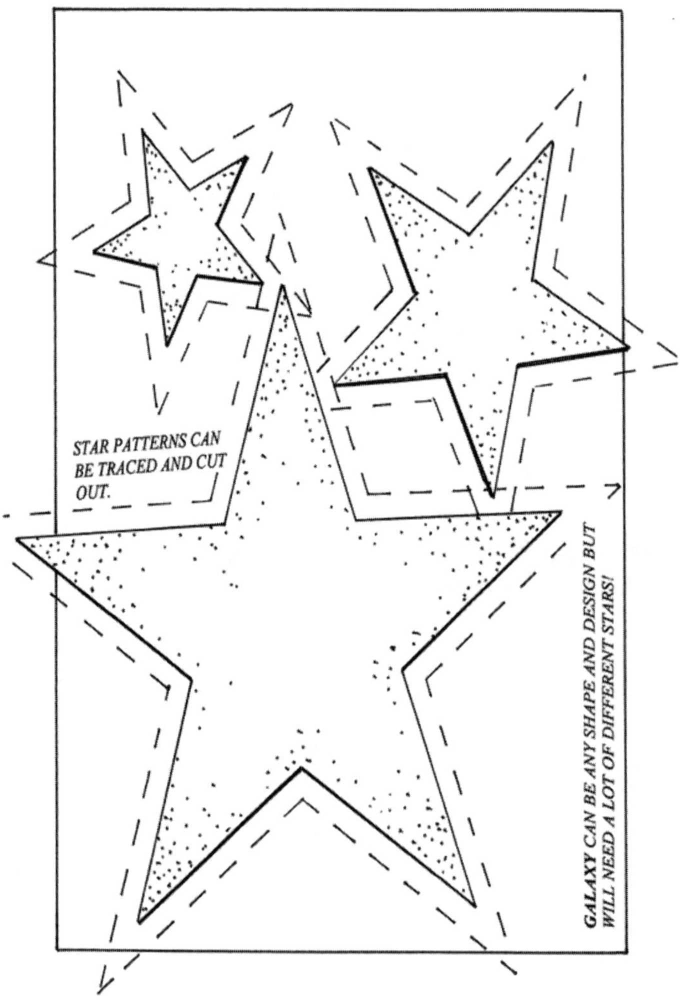

4. Lesson on PERSEVERANCE

> Tell your child that trying their very best is the true measure of success regardless of the outcome.
>
> *Coaching Tip*

PERSEVERANCE Lesson Outcomes:

- Children will write a definition of PERSEVERANCE and list some times that it would make a difference.
- Parents will give their children positive verbal reinforcement.

Parents should:

1. Reading the introductory summary on PERSEVERANCE and discuss a short definition of this indispensable value. Remember to include in this definition a list of when and where persisting would be useful.

2. Parent to Child Dialogue (positive verbal reinforcement):

✓ "Don't ever give up!"

✓ "Try it one more time."

✓ "You have the ability to do this."

✓ "I believe you can do this."

✓ "Keep on trying until you've done it."

✓ "Don't ever give up on yourself."

✓ *"Remember that this family never gives up!"*

3. **Emphasize that trying equals perseverance**. Tell your children that they should always try their best in all that they do. The risk of trying is worth the final result. Explain that when you put forth your best

effort, you have nothing to apologize for if you don't succeed. However, those who persist will find themselves winning more! By trying your best, you have truly succeeded and have the option of trying again. Getting up each morning and facing the day is the heart of perseverance. However, trying again and again after being defeated is true perseverance.

Championship Families are very good at the practice of persevering despite the odds or challenge.

PERSEVERANCE

The greatest single factor in realizing accomplishments and achievement is the steady, unrelenting power of perseverance. Persisting in a purpose, an idea or a task, despite discouragement and setbacks is difficult, but such tenacity can make the difference between success and failure. Perseverance is the reason why hopes and dreams come to life. No field of knowledge could have advanced without sheer persistence. No great scientific discovery has ever been achieved without the presence of persistence. Persisting is a powerful life strategy that can enable you and your children to realize incredible outcomes.

Often, people do not start tasks or give up using the excuses that they don't care about them, the task is far too hard or risky, or there is no way for them to be successful at completing it. These excuses mask fear of failure. Making excuses for not trying rapidly limits individual growth and greatly lowers self-esteem. Perseverance does not guarantee success but it does represent your best chance at achieving it.

❖ **Never stop trying to complete important tasks. Never forget the awesome power and brute force of PERSEVERANCE.**

NEVER GIVE UP!

PERSEVERANCE—"Try, Try Again"
T. H. Palmer
Lesson 2, McGuffey's Fourth Eclectic Reader

"T is a lesson you should heed,
Try, try again;
If at first you don't succeed,
Try, try again;
Then your courage should appear,
For, if you will persevere,
You will conquer, never fear;
Try, try again."

PERSEVERANCE—Questions:

1. What is the basic message of T.H. Palmer's poem?

2. How persistent are you in completing difficult tasks?

3. How do you handle defeats and setbacks?

4. How do you handle victories and achievements?

5. Is perseverance one of your practiced skills? Why or why not?

FAMILY ACTION PLAN ACTIVITY

> Trying doesn't mean you will always win, but it does give you the best chance at winning.
>
> ***Coaching Tip***

Children should:

- Learn about America's landing of men on the moon in 1969.
- Assemble, color and display the Saturn V rocket that took the first Americans to the Moon in 1969.
- Complete a FAMILY ACTION PLAN.

❖ **ASSIGNMENT: Teach your children about the first American Moon Landing. Help them make their Saturn V Moon Rocket and then complete an action plan.**

1. Explain how American astronauts Neil Armstrong and Buzz Aldrin's moon landing was the culmination of an ambitious "race to the moon" against the Soviet Union. The key to this American success was the effective strategy of perseverance in taking on seemingly impossible problems and meeting a demanding time schedule. Caution your children about the dangers of only going "halfway" with any project.

2. Help your children photocopy the **Saturn V Moon Rocket** sheets on heavyweight paper and assemble it by cutting out the stages and taping them together. The rocket needs to be colored with a variety of bold and creative patterns and colors. Plain white rockets are permitted. As you put the twenty-seven inch tall Saturn V (the real rocket was 363' tall!) together, remember that this was the most powerful rocket ever built.

At least twelve quotations that reflect the concept of perseverance can be written on the rocket. Once completed, the Saturn V can be displayed on a door, wall, or even suspended by a string from the ceiling.

3. Help your children complete a **FAMILY ACTION PLAN** and demonstrate how it can be used to complete projects.

• The first step is to come up with a family project that needs to be done. The project should be phrased in one complete sentence. Some examples are: planning a vacation, developing a home safety plan, remodeling the family room, landscaping the backyard and putting together a family reunion.

• Once a project is decided on, the Action Steps needed to accomplish the task are listed on the action plan template.

• Each Action Step will need to identify Persons Responsible, Specific Task, Resources Needed, Time Line and Monitoring/Report of Progress.

• Any action plan can be modified as projects continue. Some steps may need to be added or deleted.

• ***A continuing theme in any real life project is to persist until it is completed.*** *Following through is an all important activity that is vital to the ultimate success of a project. The action plan template needs to be saved and used for any future home or school project.*

Never give up!

PERSEVERANCE—***"One small step for man, one giant leap for mankind."***

Neil Armstrong as he lands on the moon (1969)

On July 20, 1969, United States astronauts Neil Armstrong and Buzz Aldrin landed on the moon. America had won the race. Armstrong later reported that he had misspoken—his original intention was to say "one small step for a man, one giant leap for mankind."

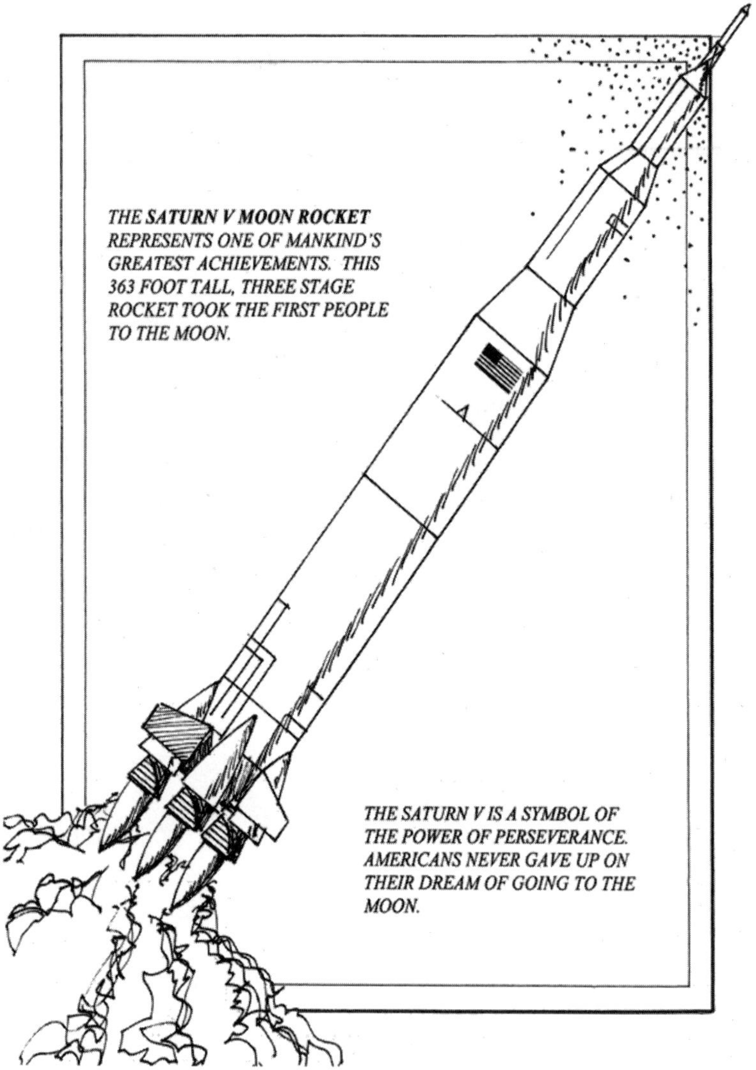
THE SATURN V MOON ROCKET REPRESENTS ONE OF MANKIND'S GREATEST ACHIEVEMENTS. THIS 363 FOOT TALL, THREE STAGE ROCKET TOOK THE FIRST PEOPLE TO THE MOON.
THE SATURN V IS A SYMBOL OF THE POWER OF PERSEVERANCE. AMERICANS NEVER GAVE UP ON THEIR DREAM OF GOING TO THE MOON.

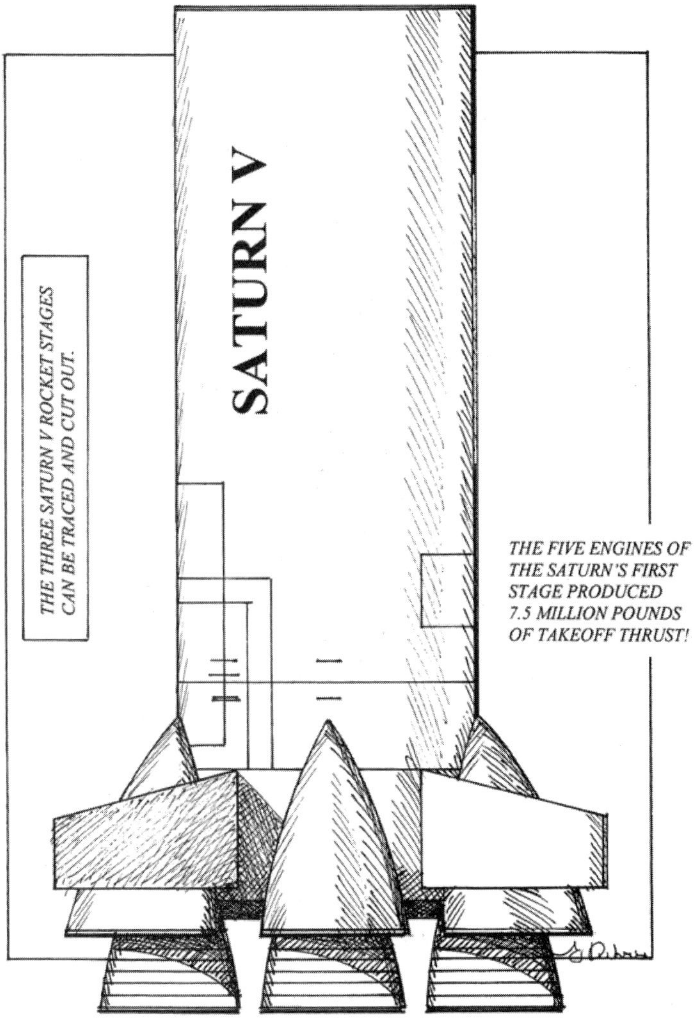
THE THREE SATURN V ROCKET STAGES CAN BE TRACED AND CUT OUT.
SATURN V
THE FIVE ENGINES OF THE SATURN'S FIRST STAGE PRODUCED 7.5 MILLION POUNDS OF TAKEOFF THRUST!

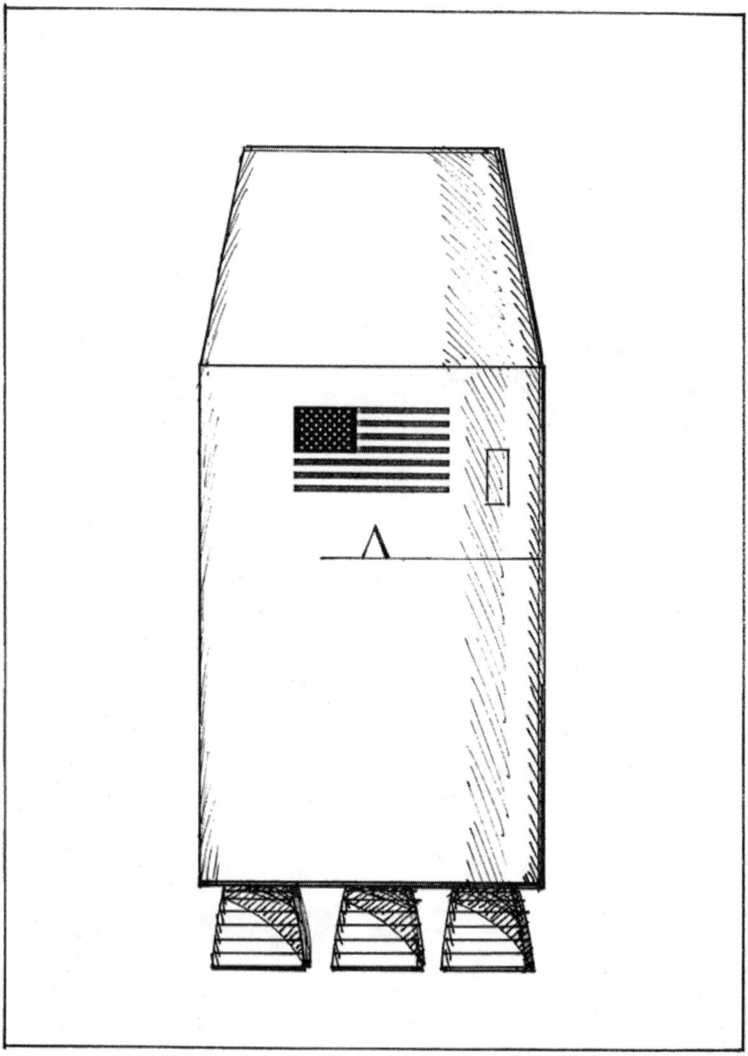

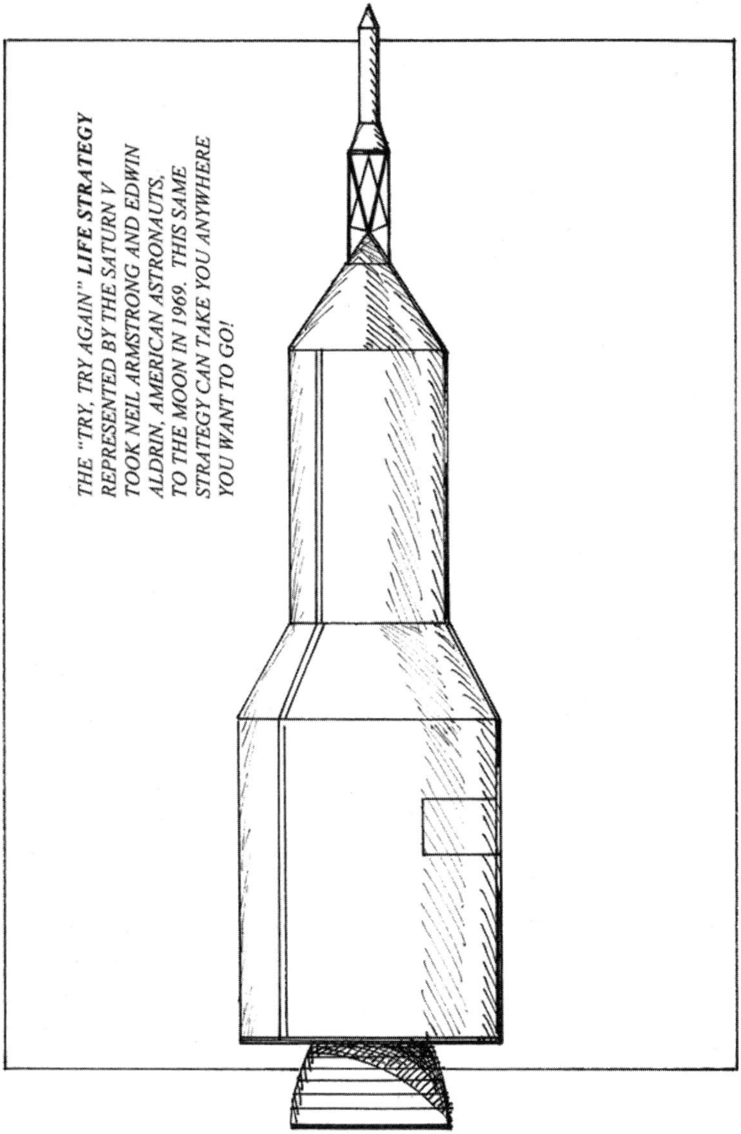
THE "TRY, TRY AGAIN" **LIFE STRATEGY**
REPRESENTED BY THE SATURN V
TOOK NEIL ARMSTRONG AND EDWIN
ALDRIN, AMERICAN ASTRONAUTS,
TO THE MOON IN 1969. THIS SAME
STRATEGY CAN TAKE YOU ANYWHERE
YOU WANT TO GO!

ACTION PLAN: ______________________

	Action Steps	Persons Responsible	Specific Task	Resources Needed	Timeline	Monitoring/ Report of Progress
1.						
2.						
3.						

	Action Steps	Persons Responsible	Specific Task	Resources Needed	Timeline	Monitoring/ Report of Progress
4.						
5.						
6.						
7.						

5. Lesson on RESPECT

> Respecting others is a basic skill; mutual respect among family members is a starting point for family growth.
>
> *Coaching Tip*

RESPECT Lesson Objectives:

- Children will write a definition of RESPECT.
- Parents will give their children positive verbal reinforcement.

Parents should:

1. Read the introductory summary on RESPECT and discuss the components of this important value. Thinking of others first is the cornerstone to fully demonstrating respect. Remind children that respect shows honor and distinction, in addition to support and commitment.

2. Parent to Child Dialogue (positive verbal reinforcement):

✓ "I respect you."

✓ "You are important to me."

✓ "You really brighten my day!"

✓ "Wow, you are incredible."

✓ "Thank you for listening to me."

✓ "I respect what you said."

✓ "I respect what you did."

RESPECT

Before you can give and expect it back from others, you have to respect yourself. Self-acceptance and self-esteem must come first before we can accept and praise others. Respect is that special stamp of approval that means we have recognized some person or some thing with honor and esteem. Respect is earned and must be mutually held between people before they can truly communicate or understand one another. Lack of respect breeds contempt and hostility.

Respect in the family is the gateway to lasting, worthwhile relationships among family members. Parents must respect their children and children must also respect their parents. It is the universal communicator of friendship; the elements of devotion and commitment. No family should ever be without the bonding power of respect and no marriage can survive long without its empowerment. Respect is a basic building block of true character.

❖ **The act of respect is much like a revolving door—what you put into it you get out of it.**

BE CONSIDERATE

RESPECT—PLEDGE OF ALLEGIANCE (1892)
James Upham and Francis Bellamy

Original 1892 Version
"I pledge allegiance to my flag
and to the republic for which
it stands, one nation, indivisible,
with liberty and justice for all."

Today's Pledge of Allegiance
"I pledge allegiance to the flag
of the United States of America
and to the republic for which
it stands, one nation, under God,
indivisible, with liberty and justice
for all."

RESPECT—Some Questions:

1.Do you know why the Pledge of Allegiance was first written in 1892?

2. In 1923 the words "my flag" were replaced with "the flag of the United States of America." Why do you think this was done?

3. In 1954 the words "under God" were added to the pledge. Why do you think this was done?

4. What are the definitions of "pledge" and "allegiance?"

5. The United States Supreme Court has ruled that no one can be forced to recite the Pledge of Allegiance. How do you feel about reciting the pledge?

FRIENDSHIP CHECKLIST ACTIVITY

> Demonstrate the qualities of being a good friend to your kids; this will help them to experience quality friendships later in life.
>
> ***Coaching Tip***

Children should:

- Answer the question "What do I value in friendships?"
- Complete a self-evaluation of yourself as a family member/friend.

❖ **ASSIGNMENT: Coach your children in some friendship's best practices. Have them discuss qualities listed on a friendship checklist and then complete a Friendship Self-Evaluation Survey.**

1. Explain how our conversation skills really rest on our ability to LISTEN to what others are saying before we think about what we are going to say. Effective communication with family and friends is directly linked to how well we listen. Remind your children that to be a friend, you must be able to listen carefully to what others are saying and respond thoughtfully and appropriately.

2. Read and discuss the "Friendship Top Twenty" checklist with your children. Review each friendship quality listed and consider if any should be taken off the list or if something should be added. Could the list be rank ordered with the most important qualities listed first and lesser ones in descending order? How should respect and listening be ranked?

3. Complete a FRIENDSHIP SELF-EVALUATION. Everyone in the family can complete this survey to determine their friendship strengths and weaknesses. A Championship Family thrives on the bonds of strong and lasting friendships. Family members should be the best of friends. These friendships form a reinforcing network that will be there in future years even when children have grown and build Championship Families of their own. Once learned, the ability to build good friendships can extend outside of the family.

The greatest outcome of a Championship Family is that family members remain good friends who are forever active in the lives of each other. Time passages, geographic separation, and circumstances are not barriers to the active friendships of family members. The bonds that forever tie extended families are in themselves important to motivating and reinforcing friendships within individual families. This strong sense of FAMILY is very much needed in today's impersonal world.

Read and discuss the Friendship Top Twenty List.

FRIENDSHIP SELF-EVALUATION

FAMILY MEMBER FRIENDSHIPS—When considering each question, use the following point scale to express your response.

5—Strongly agree!

4—Agree

3—Mostly agree

2—Partly agree

1—Do not agree

Part One

1. You consider other family members to be your best friends. ______
2. You believe that other family members consider you to be a best friend. ______
3. You feel safe and secure within your family. ______
4. The reputation of your family is important to you. ______
5. When making decisions, you consider what your family would think. ______
6. You would never do anything to hurt or upset your family. ______

Total: ______

Part Two

1. You consider yourself to be a popular person. ______
2. You like to be the center of attention. ______
3. Personal feelings are very important to you. ______
4. Whatever I need, I will do anything to get. ______
5. Your decisions are based on how they will affect you. ______
6. You rely on your own skills and resources. ______

Total: ______

THE FRIENDSHIP TOP TWENTY

1. **ADVICE** - Friends are ready to give you pointers.
2. **AVAILABILITY** - Friends are always there for you.
3. **COMMITMENT** - Friends stand with you and never leave.
4. **HONESTY** - Friends tell it like it is.
5. **HUMOR** - Friends are funny and make you laugh.
6. **EMPATHY** - Friends try and put themselves in your shoes.
7. **ENTHUSIASM** - Friends are motivated and energetic.
8. **FASHION GUIDANCE** - Friends will tell you what doesn't match.
9. **FUN FACTOR** - Friends help you relax and enjoy life.
10. **GENEROSITY** - Friends give you from the heart.
11. **GOSSIP SHARING** - Friends will share the news.
12. **LIFE-CHOICE APPROVAL** - Friends will reinforce you.
13. **LISTENING** - Friends do that when you talk.
14. **LONGEVITY** - Friends are there for a lifetime.
15. **LOYALTY** - Friends stand up for you even when you're not around.
16. **SENSE OF ADVENTURE** - Friends help you get out and explore.
17. **SENSITIVITY** - Friends are tactful.
18. **RESPECT** - Friends admire you for who you are.
19. **UNCONDITIONALITY** - Friends accept you "as is."
20. **WARMTH** - Friends have positive and caring attitudes.

Scoring: Scores of twenty-five or higher in Part One would indicate a family centered outlook and a high priority on family friendships. Of course, great friendships can exist outside the family but the rudiments of good friendships should first be learned in the family.

Scores of twenty-five or higher in Part Two would suggest a more self-centered approach to friendships. Some follow this friendship pattern which is based on selfish interests.

JOURNAL: INTRODUCTIONS

A Championship Family needs to become acquainted with itself, getting to know and appreciate every member. A family needs to realize that it is a special team of some very good people. There isn't another family quite like yours!

FAMILY JOURNAL (Title Page)

FAMILY **COAT of ARMS** and MOTTO

FAMILY **MEMBER INTRODUCTIONS**

FAMILY JOURNAL

(Family Photograph)

The

____

FAMILY

FAMILY COAT of ARMS and MOTTO (Journal Assignment: A family will design their own **Coat of Arms** and write their own **Motto**.)

FAMILY COAT of ARMS: The term "Coat of Arms" comes from medieval times when knights wore identifying cloth symbols over their armor. During the Crusades (1200's), the designing of family Coat of Arms began. Heraldry is the study of designs to distinguish individual families.

Even if you know your family has a generic Coat of Arms, it is time to design one that uniquely reflects your family. A Coat of Arms consists of a series of designs arranged on a shield representing principles and values that a family believes in or identifies with.

Using the Coat of Arms template, first select a color for each of the four quarters of the shield.

- ☐ yellow or gold—generosity
- ☐ white—peace and sincerity
- ☐ blue—loyalty and truth
- ☐ red—military fortitude
- ☐ green—hope and joy
- ☐ purple—royal majesty, sovereignty and justice

In each of the four quarters you will need to select a symbol or picture that can best express the values and practices of your family. For example, the valued trait of courage could be represented by an eagle or lion. You should consider your family traits, history, occupations, talents, hobbies, interests, accomplishments and landmarks near your home. Anything that symbolizes your family can be used. Symbols and pictures used can be drawings, photos or pictures cut out of magazines.

FAMILY MEMBER INTRODUCTIONS (Journal Assignment: Everyone will write a short introduction of themselves covering the past, present and future by completing the following information. Included are summaries of an earliest memory, a recent accomplishment and future plans/goals.)

Name: ______________________________

Birth Date: ______________________________

Birth Place: ______________________________

Father's Name: ______________________________

Mother's Name: ______________________________

The PAST

Write down the earliest memory that you can remember. It may be just a fragment or an entire event that can be shared. Thinking back to a first memory can be hard but give it a try.

The PRESENT

What recent successes and interests come to mind? This could be anything that you are proud of or something that was difficult to do. Sometimes the ordinary can be the extraordinary!

The FUTURE

What are your future plans and goals? It really makes no difference how old or young you are, everyone has or should have some "future" plans/goals. Think of what you would like to do this year or in the years to come!

SPECIAL INSTRUCTIONS: Specially design your introduction with photos, cut pictures, graphics, unique layouts and illustrations. This is your own "web page" for the Family Journal. You can use the following sample "Introduction Format" if you want.

Name: ______________________________

Birth Date: ______________________________

Birth Place: ______________________________

Father's Name: ______________________________

Mother's Name: ______________________________

(ATTACH PHOTOGRAPH)

The Past

(ATTACH PHOTOGRAPH)

The Present

(ATTACH PHOTOGRAPH)

The Future

CHAPTER TWO

CONDITIONING: (Strengths)

For family members to build and to sustain CHARACTER, they need an array of STRENGTHS. To win as a family, you must have the combined strengths of CARING, CREATIVITY, FAITH, FITNESS, LOVE, MORAL COURAGE and TRUTH. Proper CONDITIONING will give you and your children that power edge throughout life. CONDITIONING is where parents and children:

- Identify and continuously enhance overall **STRENGTHS.**
- Develop an awareness and a commitment for **CARING.**
- Become effective at demonstrating **CREATIVITY.**
- Realize how all values revolve around **FAITH.**
- Live an active life centered around habits of **FITNESS.**
- Learn how **LOVE** is life's all-conquering army.
- Develop insight into the great value of **MORAL COURAGE.**
- Understand how vital it is to honor **TRUTH** in daily living.

> Parents, you need to workout with your children in following a rigorous CONDITIONING program. The vitality and energy of a parent actively coaching their child is a requirement for a growing and strong CHARACTER. Coach and teach your children well so that they will be kind to yourself and others, reach for the stars, stay healthy, show your love in all things, hold your moral high ground, and never compromise what you know is right.
>
> ***Coaching Tip***

6. Lesson on **CARING**

> Random acts of kindness need to be your lifetime habit.
>
> *Coaching Tip*

CARING Lesson Objectives:
- Children will write a definition of CARING.
- Parents will give their children positive verbal reinforcement.

Parents should:
1. Read the introductory summary on CARING and discuss a short definition for this meaningful value. An underlying principle to caring is thinking about others and how they can be helped. Caring should be widely practiced in the home. Family members should make it a point to help each other without being asked.

2. Parent to Child Dialogue (positive verbal reinforcement):

✓ "Thank you."

✓ "Appreciate all the good things that happen to you."

✓ "Doing things for others does make you feel good."

✓ "What could you do to make him/her feel better?"

✓ "Think about what they are feeling."

✓ "Way to go, you've made a difference in helping!"

3. Opportunities for caring occur every day, and parents need to encourage their children to first notice and then do something about them. Discuss questions 1–5 about the story and caring. Caring is

showing the courage to act and thereby showing the very best of ourselves. Caring is making a great difference in the lives of others and helping us to become more complete as a person. A person rarely knows the impact that an act of kindness can have on another.

Anytime you can do something kind, you change the world around you.

CARING

When you say that you care about something, you are making a commitment that will need to be backed up with appropriate action and performance. Caring is feeling concern or empathy for others, and this means moving outside your own sphere of interests and considering the interests and well being of others. Directing your attention outward in helping and assisting others provides great opportunities for meaningful accomplishment and personal growth. Directing your attention inward in serving only your own interests limits opportunities and stunts growth. Parents need to help their children become caring people using their talents and skills for others. Children who value caring have tapped the greatest source of strength, thereby realizing immense satisfaction and achievement.

Caring unlocks the "heroic potential" in all of us and can be accomplished using these four steps:

1. Pay attention to what is going on around you and really take notice of people.
2. Treat others kindly and empathetically.
3. Don't be afraid of being criticized for your acts of kindness.
4. Start gradually as you help others by reacting to their needs and then practice increasing the scale of your assistance.

By serving others, you grow stronger. Caring reduces the friction of daily living and can give those who are defeated some motivation.

❖ **Watchfulness and conscientiousness will lead to acts of caring and kindness; this is an indicator of your personal strength and success as a person. Caring is powered by compassion and love.**

BE KIND TO YOURSELF AND OTHERS

Lesson 27, *McGuffey's Third Eclectic Reader*

THE NEW YEAR

1. One pleasant New Year morning, Edward rose, washed and dressed himself in haste. He wanted to be first to wish a "Happy New Year."

2. He looked in every room, and shouted the words of welcome. He ran into the street, to repeat them to those he might meet.

3. When he came back, his father gave him two bright, new silver dollars.

4. His face lightened up as he took them. He had wished for a long time to buy some pretty books that he had seen at the bookstore.

5. He left the house with a light heart, intending to buy the books.

6. As he ran down the street, he saw a poor German family, the father, mother, and three children shivering with cold.

7. "I wish you a Happy New Year," said Edward, as he was gaily passing on. The man shook his head.

8. "You do not belong to this country," said Edward. The man again shook his head, for he could not understand or speak our language.

9. But he pointed to his mouth, and to the children, as if to say, "These little ones have had nothing to eat for a long time."

10. Edward quickly understood that these poor people were in distress. He took out his dollars, and gave one to the man, and the other to his wife.

11. How their eyes sparkled with gratitude! They said something in their language, which doubtless meant, "We thank you a thousand times, and will remember you in our prayers."

12. When Edward came home, his father asked what books he had bought. He hung his head a moment, but quickly looked up.

13. "I have bought no books," said he, "I gave my money to some poor people, who seemed to be very hungry and wretched."

14. "I think I can wait for my books till next New Year. Oh, if you have seen how glad they were to receive the money!"

15. "My dear boy," said his father, "here is a whole bundle of books. I give them to you, more as a reward for your goodness of heart than as a New Year gift."

16. "I saw you give the money to the poor German family. It was no small sum for a little boy to give cheerfully."

17. "Be thus ever ready to help the poor, and wretched, and distressed; and every year of your life will be to you a Happy New Year."

CARING—Questions:

1. What was Edward's attitude when his father gave him two silver dollars?

2. How did Edward feel about the poor German family that he met?

3. How did Edward explain giving his money away?

4. Was Edward happy about what he had done?

5. What did Edward's father do? Why did he do this?

THANK YOU CARD ACTIVITY

> Teach your children the importance of kindness and gratitude, train them of the necessity to always say THANK YOU!
>
> *Coaching Tip*

The two words that you cannot say enough are "thank you." This should be said or written with a conviction which underscores that you really mean what you are saying. Children need to learn that these two words should be an automatic reflex response for any act of kindness or thoughtfulness that comes their way. Simply put, you are repaying kindness with kindness.

❖ **ASSIGNMENT: Help your children design ten special thank you note cards and then send them.**

1. When should a thank you note be sent?
Thank you notes must be sent for any significant gift that you receive, when you stay at someone's house as a guest, and when you feel the need to appreciate someone special. Thank you notes should be sent for acts of kindness, for someone being very helpful, appreciation for things that have been done over a period of time, and for a job well done. Thank you notes can be sent anytime you want to express a special thanks to someone for their help in the past, present and future.

2. What should a thank you note look like?
Thank you notes can take many different forms, but the card should match what was received as a gift, act of kindness or service. The thank you note cards that you will be designing will all be done by hand and will contain handwritten messages when they are used. While thank you messages can be typed, emailed or even faxed, there is nothing that can replace the impact of those done by hand and mailed. Parents need to stress the importance of the personal touch even in this world

of advancing technology. Handwriting carries a special message that you are showing your level of caring by taking the time to personally write a note of thanks.

Some guidelines when writing thank you notes:

- Use a special heavyweight card paper for your thank you cards so that they can be folded and placed in an envelope.
- The outside of the card can be a drawing or design. Use of color is encouraged.
- Stickers or photographs from magazines can be used to decorate the card.
- All of the cards should be done differently.
- The inside of the card will be blank and ready for your handwritten message of thanks.
- Thank you messages can be short or long. Children should be told that their feelings of kindness and gratitude will be their best guide to what they are going to say.

Children can write family and friends a message on the card, thanking them for something that they have done recently or in the past. Have your kids send two or three thank you notes right away. Encourage them to keep their thank you cards ready for special occasions when they might be needed. More can always be made!

Children should be reminded that sending thank you cards and notes should be a lifetime habit that shows a caring and appreciative attitude.

> Even in this rapidly changing century, there is something very special in receiving a handmade thank you card with a handwritten note in the mail from family or friends. That's caring!
>
> *Coaching Tip*

Thank You
THANK YOU
THANK YOU
Thank You
THANK YOU!
Thank You

7. Lesson on **CREATIVITY**

> Children are very creative. Give them chances to demonstrate it.
>
> *Coaching Tip*

CREATIVITY Lesson Objectives:

- Children will write a definition of CREATIVITY.
- Parents will give their children positive verbal reinforcement.

Parents should:

1. Read the introductory summary on CREATIVITY and discuss a short definition for this imaginative value with your child. It is important for you as the parent to fan the sparks of creativity that your children display. Creativity thrives in a nurturing and supportive environment providing the necessary materials and time. Parents can do much to open the door of creativity for their kids. Children should realize that being creative is really solving problems with new and fresh ideas.

Creativity is being original in thought and expression.

2. Parent to Child Dialogue (positive verbal reinforcement):

✓ "Dream of things that never were."

✓ "That's really creative."

✓ "I would never have thought of that!"

✓ "You will think of something."

✓ "You have a wonderful imagination."

✓ "What a great idea!"

✓ "I am very impressed with what you have created."

3. Dreaming something up and inventing new things are what inquiring minds can do. That's why it is important for parents to encourage their children to ask lots of questions. Asking questions should become a lifetime habit. Every effort should be made to find good answers for the questions of children. And if you as the parent cannot readily answer all of your children's questions, look up the answers with them. Training your child to look for answers and knowing where to find them is a valuable life and work skill.

Ideas are much like plants as they need constant attention, patience and caring to grow and flourish.

CREATIVITY

Being creative is a capacity that some people seemingly have more than others. Creativity, or using the limitless power of imagination, lives in all of us; building new ideas and concepts is something you can do and so can your kids. Creativity is a wonderful avenue that can allow us to escape the usual and embrace original and ingenious applications. Everyone needs to look beyond the traditional and "think outside the box" to see what is not there.

We all tend to spend a great deal of time dwelling in our own comfort zones where routine habits rule. Thinking of something new and different is often seen as threatening. Staying on the beaten path is seemingly the safest way to go, but Championship Families like to blaze new trails. Rigidity of mind and spirit is alien to creativity where an open and curious mind must be able to veer off the path and explore the countryside. Values give creativity purpose and focus leading to quality solutions and production. Character values have the power to unleash the "empire of the mind" to unimaginably high levels of creativity, thereby producing significant works that are deeply satisfying to the individual as well as being worthy of possible admiration and acclaim from others. Don't be afraid to let your creativity flow.

❖ **Imagine all the possibilities! Use your talents and skills to their maximum potential as you push your vision to reach boldly over the horizon. It is all there, you just have to see it!**

"**DREAM** OF WONDERS . . .
EXPLORE YOUR WORLD . . .
PURSUE YOUR TALENTS . . .
STRETCH YOURSELF . . .
SOAR TO YOUR DESTINY . . .
INVENT FROM WITHIN . . .
VISUALIZE THE UNSEEN . . .
ACHIEVE THE INCREDIBLE . . .
REALIZE YOUR TRUE EMPIRE . . ."

Coaching Tip

CREATIVITY—"I Will Think of It"
Lesson 39, McGuffey's Third Eclectic Reader

I WILL THINK OF IT
1. "I will think of it." It is easy to say this; but do you know what great things have come from thinking?

2. We can not see our thoughts, or hear, or taste, or feel them; and yet what mighty power they have!

3. Sir Isaac Newton was seated in his garden on a summer's evening, when he saw an apple fall from a tree. He began to *think*, and, in trying to find out why the apple fell, discovered how the earth, sun, moon, and stars are kept in their places.

4. A boy named James Watt sat quietly by the fireside, watching the lid of the tea- kettle as it moved up and down. He began to *think*; he wanted to find out why the steam in the kettle moved the heavy lid.

5. From that time he went on thinking, and thinking; and when he became a man, he improved the steam engine so much that it could with the greatest ease, do the work of many horses.

6. When you see a steamboat, a steam mill, or a locomotive, remember that it would never have been built if it had not been for the hard thinking of someone.

7. James Ferguson was a poor Scotch shepherd boy. Once, seeing the inside of a watch, he was filled with wonder. "Why should I not make a watch?" thought he.

8. But how was he to get the materials out of which to make the wheels and the mainspring? He soon found how to get them: he made the mainspring out of a piece of whalebone. He then made a wooden clock which kept good time.

9. He began, also, to copy pictures with a pen, and portraits with oil colors. In a few years, while still a small boy, he earned money enough to support his father.

10. When he became a man, he went to London to live. Some of the wisest men in England, and the king himself, used to attend his lectures. His motto was, "I will think of it;" and he made his thoughts useful to himself and the world.

CREATIVITY—Questions:

1. What started Sir Isaac Newton thinking about gravity?

2. What started James Watt thinking about steam engines?

3. What was James Ferguson's motto?

4. Do you have faith in your own ability to think of new things?

5. Are you effective in applying what you have learned to new situations?

NEW INVENTIONS ACTIVITY

> A child needs to learn that good ideas have great power. Encourage them to use their creativity in pursuit of theirs!
>
> *Coaching Tip*

Children should:

- Learn about some of the major inventions of the 20th century.
- List all of the inventions they can find in your home.
- Dream up an invention and write a patent for it.

❖ **ASSIGNMENT: Assist your child in considering past inventions and help them to write a "patent" for a new one.**

1. **The 20th century witnessed an incredible number of new inventions and discoveries that have greatly changed how we live.** Some of these inventions and scientific breakthroughs have included:

☐ AIRPLANE 1903
☐ AUTOMOBILE ASSEMBLY LINE 1914
☐ COMMERCIAL RADIO 1920s
☐ TELEVISION 1930s
☐ JET AIRCRAFT 1937
☐ ATOMIC BOMB 1945
☐ NUCLEAR POWER 1950s
☐ MICROWAVE 1945
☐ TRANSISTOR 1947
☐ POLIO VACCINE 1955
☐ EARTH SATELLITE 1957
☐ INTERNET 1969
☐ PERSONAL COMPUTERS 1970s
☐ STEALTH AIRCRAFT 1980s
☐ ARTIFICIAL HEART 1982
☐ CELL PHONES 1990s

Select five of the above inventions that you consider to be the most significant, and then work with your child to find the answers to the following questions.

- What was achieved?
- Who was involved in its invention?
- What impact did the event have?

2. **Go through your house and work with your children to compile a list of all the inventions that you can find.** Consider all the appliances and furniture in the house. Practically everything you see in your house is an invention of some kind. Consider those things that you can't see as you go through each room including the electrical, heating, cooling and the plumbing systems. A house contains literally hundreds of different inventions.

3. **Decide on a new invention that could change the world and then complete a U.S. Patent application for it.** Considering past inventions can help in thinking up new ones. An invention can be a device, process or product. Your new invention must somehow be beneficial and cannot in any way be harmful, such as a weapon of war.

The following fields can be researched in determining what has been invented and what other inventions could be useful.

- AGRICULTURE
- COMMUNICATIONS
- HOME & FAMILY LIFE
- MEDICINE
- SCIENCE & TECHNOLOGY
- TRANSPORTATION

In deciding upon a new invention, consider what it will do and how it will work. Be sure and give your invention an original and imaginative name.

U.S. Patents were started in 1790 when President George Washington signed the first one. That year, patents were given for an improvement in the potash fertilizer, a new way to make candles, and an upgraded flour-milling machine. Today, millions of patents later, new ones are applied for daily as our increasingly technological world continues to spiral upward in a sharply rising curve.

U.S. PATENT APPLICATION

1. Briefly explain what your invention does. What do you call it?

2. Give a description of your invention. List the basic specifications for your invention.

3. List everything that your new invention can do and how it works. These are your claims.

4. Make a simple drawing or diagram of your invention:

_______________________________ _______________________

Name of inventor Date

8. Lesson on **FAITH**

> I believe parents should show that character is grounded in a deeply held faith in God.
>
> ***Coaching Tip***

FAITH Lesson Objectives:
- Children will write a definition of FAITH.
- Parents will give their children positive verbal reinforcement.

Parents should
1. Read the introductory summary on FAITH and discuss which parts should be included in a definition of this most vital value. It is my belief that faith sets us on a firm and steady course to follow while lack of faith cuts us loose to wander in search of where we should go in life and why. As a follower of God, I feel faithfulness requires a bold statement that makes a clear commitment and belief in God's word. I think Championship Families find their greatest strength in the word of God.

2. Parent to Child Dialogue for followers of Christianity and Catholicism (positive verbal reinforcement):

✓ "God's love and faithfulness will never leave you."

✓ "Believe with all your heart."

✓ "Life is not chance but design."

✓ "Trust in God."

✓ "You are what you deeply believe in."

✓ "God loves you."

✓ "Faith will always overpower worry or doubt."

3. A positive, religious activity for families of Christianity and Catholicism would be to discuss how the Bible is so important in developing a strong FAITH in God. I would recommend answering questions 1–5, and explain how wisdom is tightly intertwined with faith.

It is my interpretation that:

- **Wisdom** is the life skill that you display in following moral principles honoring God. Wisdom is the consistent application of faith.
- **Faith** is the daily practice of believing in God and being wise in the eyes of the Lord. Faith is simply to believe in God.

FAITH

I feel that faith can be seen to have many different dimensions—from a person with complete confidence in themselves, a belief in an idea or thing, to the conviction that the will and power of God is paramount in life. My assessment is that faith is a powerful force that can greatly empower us in our daily walks, but that faith must be firmly centered on God. To those who are followers, such faith will help strengthen our ability to perform and to handle problems. It is my opinion that having a strong faith in the Lord empowers us to fully develop our character and wisdom to its fullest extent.

To me, Christian faithfulness carries the confidence and trust of God. I feel the right call is to ground your faith in the Lord and build this value every day of your life. For some who choose these practices, it may be difficult in a material and selfish world but one that requires hard work and brave allegiance. It is my opinion that faith is everything.

❖ **For those that follow the Bible, Faith in God gives power and peace in your life. Your strength of character is reinforced and unleashed when you feel that your life has a higher purpose and plan.**

TRUST IN GOD

FAITH—PROLOGUE TO BOOK of PROVERBS
Proverbs 1 : 1-9, The BIBLE

1 The proverbs of Solomon son of David, king of Israel:
2 for attaining wisdom and discipline;
for understanding words of insight;
3 for acquiring a disciplined and prudent life,
doing what is right and just and fair;
4 for giving prudence to the simple,
knowledge and discretion to the young –
5 let the wise listen and add to their learning,
and let the discerning get guidance –

FAITH—Questions:

1. Who was Solomon in the Bible?

2. Where do you place your faith? Why?

3. How are faith and wisdom alike and different?

4. Why does it take faith to have wisdom?

5. How familiar are you with the Bible? Do you have an understanding of the Old and New Testaments?

BIBLE CUBE ACTIVITY

> Parents, your faith in words and deeds will be a roadmap for your children.
>
> *Coaching Tip*

I feel that family is where Faith will make an incredible difference in how parents and children interact and prosper. Faith helps a family literally "take root." Parents and children alike need the reassurance that they are protected and have a destiny to fulfill. Taking root does not happen by itself. This process is faith driven, and families that achieve this are indeed champions.

❖ **ASSIGNMENT: I believe a positive, enriching activity for followers of the Bible would be to teach your child about the Ten Commandments and help them to construct a Bible Cube.**

"The longest journey a person can take is the twelve inches from the head to the heart," an old proverb says. Who is helping our children to make this journey? In Western civilization, many have followed the Ten Commandments. Some children are taught the Commandments so early and so thoroughly that they sink to the bottom of the child's mind, where everything that comes along later settles on them.

Every year legislators write and pass more state and Federal laws, and even more interpretations of those laws. In my opinion, what a family needs to know to live a balanced, fruitful life is contained in ten simply worded direct laws.

Becoming familiar with verses from the Bible is extremely important in building faith in a family. **I think** every member of the family should have their own Bible and spend time exploring and reading from it. The Bible is the highest bestselling book in history, and knowledge of its contents is vitally important to a devoted believer. I would suggest as an introduction that parents discuss the Bible's table of contents with their children from the Old Testament to the New Testament.

Help your child put together a BIBLE CUBE that is made out of heavy paper card stock. The cube will include four Bible verses along with the Lord's Prayer, Matthew 6:9-13. Verses that are used for the cube should be memorized. Children can write additional Bible verses on index cards kept in a file box simply entitled, "Faith."

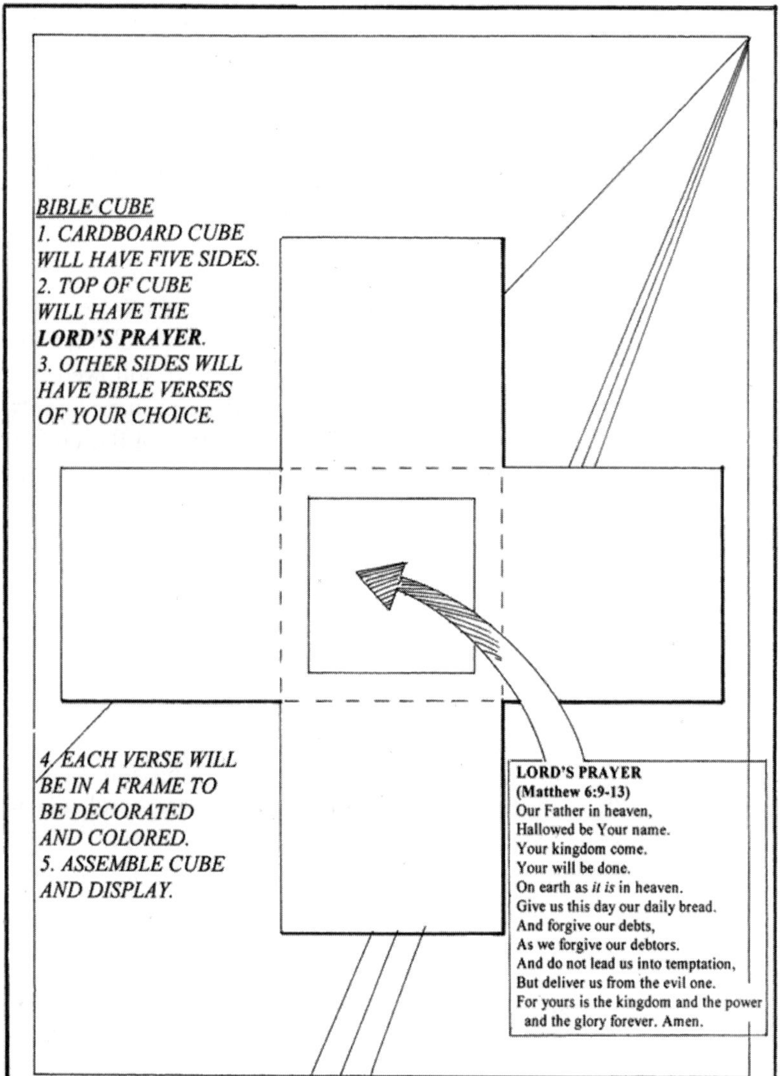
BIBLE CUBE
1. CARDBOARD CUBE WILL HAVE FIVE SIDES.
2. TOP OF CUBE WILL HAVE THE LORD'S PRAYER.
3. OTHER SIDES WILL HAVE BIBLE VERSES OF YOUR CHOICE.
4. EACH VERSE WILL BE IN A FRAME TO BE DECORATED AND COLORED.
5. ASSEMBLE CUBE AND DISPLAY.
LORD'S PRAYER
(Matthew 6:9-13)
Our Father in heaven,
Hallowed be Your name.
Your kingdom come.
Your will be done.
On earth as it is in heaven.
Give us this day our daily bread.
And forgive our debts,
As we forgive our debtors.
And do not lead us into temptation,
But deliver us from the evil one.
For yours is the kingdom and the power and the glory forever. Amen.

9. Lesson on FITNESS

> A healthy lifestyle that includes proper diet, regular exercise and enough rest will help sustain habits of good character.
>
> ***Coaching Tip***

FITNESS Lesson Objectives:

- Children will write a definition of FITNESS.
- Parents will give their children positive verbal reinforcement .

Parents should:

1. Read the introductory summary on FITNESS and discuss a short definition for this vital and sustaining value with your child. Good health is the ready companion of an active and alert mind. The three elements of a healthy lifestyle—diet, exercise and rest -need to be a part of your definition. Children need to be encouraged to maintain an active and healthy lifestyle throughout their lives. Participants in life always learn more and have more fun.

2. Parent to Child Dialogue (positive verbal reinforcement):

✓ "I enjoyed walking with you."

✓ "Thank you for finishing all of your vegetables and fruit."

✓ "You look very rested today."

✓ "Good for you for choosing water over soda!"

✓ "Come on let's exercise together!"

✓ "I had fun playing soccer with you at the park."

✓ "Good job on always having such a good breakfast."

3. Discuss how avoiding physical exercise is the result of excuses, which is why a positive acceptance of exercise is very important. Discuss questions 1–5 and how regular exercise can happen as a result of the "right attitude." It is especially important for children to be physically active and adopt this practice as a lifelong habit. The strategies for winning the "battle of the bulge" should start in childhood.

To encourage physical activity in children, make such experiences FUN! Make physical activity a regular family activity. Lead by example as your eating, exercising, and sleeping routines will not go unnoticed by your children. You must "walk the talk."

The eyes of your children are upon you, your behaviors and lifestyle. Send them a compelling and persuasive message.

FITNESS

Fitness is looking and feeling good due to healthy habits. This helps a person to sustain effective performance for prolonged periods of time, even under adverse conditions. Having physical and mental conditioning to withstand the onslaught of daily tasks and problems is a basic requirement of a Championship Family. If children don't have the energy or the will to push ahead, their character values will suffer. All family members are at their best when they feel good and are energetic. Fitness comes from three good health habits: 1. EATING RIGHT, 2. REGULAR EXERCISE, and 3. GETTING REST.

Life's cutting edge is measured in your total fitness which is expressed through physical and mental stamina. These two qualities enhance you and your values. Fitness requires daily effort, and many people tend to take their health for granted by excessively eating, avoiding exercise, and skimping on sleep. The results are damaging health and longevity. Health is your children's bridge to hope and when they have that, they have everything.

❖ **Good health is the engine that will power you through life. A healthy lifestyle based on sufficient nutrition, exercise, and rest enables everyone to perform at their maximum potential.**

STAY HEALTHY FOR LIFE

Eat the BIG FIVE every day:
1. FRUITS
2. VEGETABLES
3. BEANS
4. NUTS/SEEDS
5. WHOLE GRAINS

FITNESS—"Lazy Ned"
Lesson 7, McGuffey' s Fourth Eclectic Reader

LAZY NED

1. "'Tis royal fun," cried lazy Ned,
"To coast upon my fine, new sled,
And beat the other boys;
But then, I can not bear to climb
The tiresome hill, for every time
It more and more annoys."

2. So, while his schoolmates glided by,
And gladly tugged uphill, to try
Another merry race,
Too indolent to share their plays,
Ned was compelled to stand and gaze,
While shivering in his place.

3. Thus, he would never take the pains
To seek the prize that labor gains,
Until the time has passed;

For, all his life, he dreaded still
The silly bugbear* of *uphill*,
And died a dunce at last.

*Bugbear—something frightful.

Questions:

1. What did Ned say was fun and not fun?

2. Why didn't Ned take part in the sledding with the others?

3. What was Ned's fate?

4. Are you fit enough to "take the pain to seek the prize?"

5. What are you doing to keep yourself physically fit and ready to live an active life?

4-WEEK CHALLENGE ACTIVITY

> When family members are physically fit, they feel like champions and that makes all the difference.
>
> ***Coaching Tip***

The road to physical fitness begins with wanting to be in better shape, having a plan to get there and then getting there! Parents need to take care of themselves, energize their family relationships and take care of their children. All this takes energy, which comes from getting and staying in good shape. And being physically fit applies to the entire family. All members should keep themselves in good shape. Championship Families keep themselves fit. Healthy people are happy people regardless of their age. Healthy people are those who know about and practice good nutrition, get adequate rest and maintain a schedule of regular exercise. Fitness must be a life-long commitment.

❖ ASSIGNMENT: **Parents, you and your children will define some key fitness terms and complete the 4-WEEK CHALLENGE.**

1. **Help your children define:**
   - **Aerobic endurance**
   - **Pulse rate**
   - **Aerobic conditioning activities**
   - **Muscular strength**
   - **Muscle**
   - **Weight training**
   - **Ligaments and Tendons**
   - **Calories**
   - **Proteins**
   - **Vitamins**
   - **Carbohydrates**
   - **Minerals**

2. **Participate with your child in the 4-WEEK CHALLENGE**. Using the **FITNESS CHALLENGE CARD**, parents and their children will record their health practices earning FITNESS POINTS over a four week period in seven categories. If anyone has any health problems or concerns, a doctor should be consulted before undertaking any fitness or physical conditioning program. No one should push themselves or take any unnecessary risks during the 4-Week Challenge. Everyone keeps their own card.

> Fitness helps build self-esteem for everyone in the family.
>
> *Coaching Tip*

Daily Scoring for **FITNESS POINTS**:

SMART EATING

For eating one serving of the Big Five (Fruits, Vegetables, Beans, Nuts/Seeds and Whole Grains), you earn one point for each day up to seven points for the week.

WATER INTAKE

For drinking a daily minimum of five 12-ounce glasses of water/juice/milk, you earn one point per day up to seven for the week.

SLEEPING LOG

For getting seven hours or more of sleep, you earn one point per day up to seven for the week.

WALKING LOG

For walking one mile—two points. Walking at least half a mile but under a mile equals one point. Walking at least three times a week is recommended. Always exercise safety when walking—walk during the day and in places that you trust. It is better for the whole family to walk together.

PUSH UP CHART

For doing ten or more push-ups (can be traditional military-style or bent knee), one point per day for up to seven for the week

F-I-T BONUS

Any additional exercise activity that could include a sports practice or event will earn five bonus points.

WEEKLY FAMILY-SPORTS EVENT

This could include any sports activity in which the entire family participates: Biking, tag football, miniature golf; bowling, soccer, frisbee throwing, basketball, tennis, swimming, skiing, volleyball and the list goes on. This activity earns all participants ten points.

At the end of four weeks, the **FITNESS CHALLENGE CARDS** will be scored and various awards distributed to all who participated (see sample card on page 68). Parents need to determine what individual and family rewards should be given. Some of these healthy activities might become ongoing and practiced for a lifetime. This 4-Week Challenge could be repeated at different times throughout the year.

The key to eating right, resting and exercising is enjoying all these activities and having fun realizing that your own personal health is only your number one priority. Without good health, everything you hope to accomplish in life is at risk.

FITNESS CHALLENGE CARD
4-WEEK CHALLENGE

Name: ______________________________

Date started: ______________ Date completed: ______________

	Week 1	Week 2	Week 3	Week 4	Totals
Smart eating	______	______	______	______	______
Water intake	______	______	______	______	______
Sleeping log	______	______	______	______	______
Walking log	______	______	______	______	______
Push-up chart	______	______	______	______	______
F-I-T bonus	______	______	______	______	______
Weekly family sports event	______	______	______	______	______

Grand total ______

Never stop taking the 4-WEEK CHALLENGE.

10. Lesson on **LOVE**

> Love is your mightiest of engines, maintain it well throughout the years.
>
> *Coaching Tip*

LOVE Lesson Objectives:
- Children will write a definition of LOVE.
- Parents will give their children positive verbal reinforcement.

Parents should:
1. Read the introductory summary on LOVE and discuss the powerful ingredients that comprise the meaning of love. Parents need to point out that love is the greatest of motivators and that its application is vital to living life to its fullest. Tell your child that your love for them is truly unconditional and will always be there for them. Explain that many times love can include sacrifice, as a parent, means putting the welfare of their children above their own interests.

2. Parent to Child Dialogue (positive verbal reinforcement):

✓ "I love you."

✓ "Tell me how you are feeling?"

✓ "While you were gone, I was thinking about you."

✓ "I will always be there for you."

✓ "You are constantly in my thoughts and prayers."

✓ "You are very important to me."

3. Discuss the special qualities of love, and then questions 1–5 with your children. Explain that love is an all-important lifelong habit.

Explain that when you care about someone, you will make sacrifices for them. Show how love among family members is the tie that will forever bind and hold a family together. Love in the family is an unconditional practice that is established from the first beginnings through the lives of all its members. There is no substitute for the presence of love between family members.

Love in the family is what will give incredible strength and vitality.

Love in the family is at the beginning and end everlasting.

Love in the family gives it that "championship" dimension.

LOVE

Make no mistake about the power of love throughout a person's life. Love reaches boldly across the experience of life, embracing all aspects of people's lives including love of learning. People can love each other as well as what they are doing with their skills and talents. The important thing is to fill your life with love, not indifference, with passion, not apathy regarding persons, places, activities, knowledge, and virtue. Love is an awakening and expression of mighty forces which must be pursued with enthusiasm. Love is real. Love is CHARACTER PARENTING.

A parent shows love in manifold ways and a direct expression of such love is spending quality time with their children. Time is a treasure, so spend it lavishly on those you love. Reading to your young children is a prime example of showing your love and instilling a love of learning at the same time. There is no greater gift of learning than to model and practice active reading. Above all else, love and honor your children with passion and dedication. Love your children unconditionally.

❖ **Love can propel you to incredible heights and happiness.**

SHOW YOUR LOVE IN ALL THINGS

> Don't forget that pets can be an important component of love in the family.
>
> *Coaching Tip*

LOVE—THE LOVE CHAPTER
1 Corinthians 13: 1-13, The BIBLE

13 1. If I speak in the tongues of men and angles, but have not love, I am only a resounding gong or a clanging cymbal.

2. If I have the gift of prophecy and can fathom all mysteries and all knowledge, and if I have faith that can move mountains, but have not love, I am nothing.

3. If I give all I possess to the poor and surrender my body to the flames, but have not love, I gain nothing.

4. Love is patient, love is kind. It does not envy, it does not boast, it is not proud.

5. It is not rude, it is not self-seeking, it is not easily angered, it keeps no record of wrongs.

6. Love does not delight in evil but rejoices with the truth.

7. It always protects, always trusts, always hopes, always perseveres.

8. Love never fails. But when there are prophecies, they will cease; where there are tongues, they will be stilled; where there is knowledge, it will pass away.

9. Now we see but a poor reflection as in a mirror; then we see face to face. Now I know in part; then I shall know fully, even as I am fully known.

10. And now these three remain: faith, hope and love. But the greatest of these is love.

LOVE—Questions:

1. In 1 Corinthians 13: 1-13, how important is love?

2. What are the qualities of love that are described in this passage of the Bible?

3. How does love give protection to the family?

4. How do parents show their love for their children?

5. How can children show their love for their parents?

FAMILY TRADITIONS ACTIVITY

> The family is where love begins and thrives; good family times are the greatest of times.
>
> *Coaching Tip*

The family is where love and appreciation forever bind all members together. Parents who develop families strong in love have met the number one requirement of character parenting. Making a house a home is a primary family goal. In a home, you feel the warming presence of love and appreciation. Parents have the leadership role in building families that are strong in character values. This involves character parenting and coaching as a family grows and grows. A parent must strive to make their family home the best it can be—a place where love is present twenty four hours a day, seven days a week. This is the Love 24/7 Rule.

❖ **ASSIGNMENT: Have all of your family members participate in the FAMILY TRADITIONS activity.**

A family isn't just some people sharing the same house together, but a loving and interacting group who are actively involved in making their home a great place to be. The following activities can be accomplished by families with elementary to high school age children. These activities are all about building family traditions and rituals that will forever go on in time and underscore the power of character parenting. Traditions bring a family together and bond its members in experiences and memories, passing down values from one generation to another.

> The bond of love is forged through building and experiencing the many traditions of a family.
>
> *Coaching Tip*

HOLD A FAMILY MEETING

Use the FAMILY MEETING MINUTES form as your guide to holding family meetings. Having regular weekly meetings is something that can become a family tradition. The basic purpose of the meeting is to plan a calendar and organize for the **Adventure Day, Arts and Crafts Night, Game Night** and **Family Dinner.**

- Schedule the family meeting at a specific time and place. Make sure there will be no interruptions or distractions that will interfere with the meeting.

- Many meetings will be needed to plan everything, so have fun with them.
- The roles of Chair and Secretary can be taken by the parents initially but, with time and experience, these roles can be taken on by the children. Other roles can be assigned that could include an Assistant Chair, Sergeant-At-Arms, Coordinator, Parliamentarian or any other position that you can think of.
- Meetings will be more enjoyable if they include some planned refreshments.
- Post meeting notices (Date, Time, and Location) on the refrigerator and maintain a Family Suggestion Box—read all suggestions at meetings and discuss them.

ADVENTURE DAY

This is a day where the family goes somewhere together just to have FUN! The sky is the limit in making this day one to remember.

- A park, beach, mountains, desert, river, creek, museum, theater, sports venue . . . any place that looks like a fun place to go is a possibility.
- Everyone needs to have a voice in where to go. A wise Chair will successfully guide the family to a good decision.
- Plan to take lots of pictures.
- In planning this activity, assign everyone a responsibility and develop a checklist of things that need to be done.
- This activity can become a regular monthly family ritual.

ARTS & CRAFTS NIGHT

This activity can involve everyone working together on an arts and crafts activity. No television or Internet activity will be allowed.

- A specific time needs to be scheduled along with planning and organizing the project to be completed.
- Simple handicraft projects using construction paper and colored markers can be used in making placemats that could be laminated.

- Various hobbies ranging from collections of things, do-it-yourself projects, the arts (drawing, music, drama, writing) and games could be explored.
- A family mural could be designed with each family member, completing a section or panel over several sessions. Finished work could be framed and displayed.
- Handicraft skills or interest in a hobby could well be encouraged through periodic family arts and crafts activity nights.

GAME NIGHT

The focus of this activity is to have all family members participate in playing a board/card game or putting a puzzle together.

- Any game that uses a board like "Monopoly" or cards like "Balderdash" can be played.
- Puzzles are also good choices. Choose a puzzle that will interest everyone. Anything from 500 to 1,000 pieces will work.
- Whatever game is played, plan to have refreshments and allow enough time to finish the activity.
- Laughing and even occasional yelling is permitted!
- Families should have a game and puzzle library ready to use. If not, assemble one.

FAMILY DINNER

A seemingly endangered species is the family dinner. The dinner table has long been the traditional place where families bonded, shared, communicated, informed, persuaded, debated, celebrated, entertained, laughed and networked. Dinnertime is the time and place where the American family can come together. The final activity is to have a special Family Dinner.

- Set aside a specific date and time for this dinner. Make a big deal out of it.
- Assign family members roles in planning the menu, shopping for food, decorating the table, preparing the food, serving and cleanup.

- Serve a family favorite dish that everyone likes.
- Prepare a specially printed dinner menu and have one at everyone's plate.
- Use the best china and silverware.
- Have everyone dress up a little.
- Have a special centerpiece decoration perhaps with flowers.
- Make the dinner special by adding candles and some background music. No television or videos can be on.
- Conversation will include past family stories recalled, current family events and future family plans. In short, dinner conversation will focus on the family.
- Have an incredibly delicious dessert. You can't practice the "Big Five" all the time. (See FITNESS)
- Another good activity would be to have family members exchange thank you cards recognizing appreciation for past help and encouragement.

HOLIDAY TRADITIONS

Suggestions:

- Taking the family to a pumpkin patch to select a pumpkin.
- Family pumpkin carving and decorating contest.
- Assigning Thanksgiving dinner jobs from helping with grocery shopping to final clean up.
- Having all family members give thanks during the prayer before the Thanksgiving dinner.
- Selecting decorations for the family holiday.
- Singing and celebrating with other families.
- Donating new toys and clothes as in "Toys for Tots."
- Making and mailing other family members holiday cards.
- Helping decorate the house for holidays and New Year's.
- Taking special drives around the neighborhood to view decorations.
- Reading and sharing stories.

The outcome of these activities is for a family to experience and enjoy one another in more planned situations. Interactive families communicate better and appreciate one another more fully, thereby building stronger relationships. They can explore common interests producing strong and lasting memories of being together and having fun. Character parenting comes alive in the setting of a functional and dynamic family doing things together and forever bonding.

> Lackadaisical families avoid adventure and discovery while Championship Families avidly explore together, seeking new horizons.
>
> *Coaching Tip*

FAMILY MEETING MINUTES

Meeting called to order: ______________________________

(Date and Time)

Family members present: ______________________________

____

____

Reading and Approval of Past Minutes: ____________________

Reports:

NEW Business:

OLD Next Business:

Next meeting scheduled for: ___________________________

Meeting adjourned at: ________________________________

Respectively submitted,

____

11. Lesson on MORAL COURAGE

> To be brave is good, but to be morally brave is true EXCELLENCE.
>
> *Coaching Tip*

MORAL COURAGE Lesson Objectives:

- Children will write a definition of MORAL COURAGE.
- Parents will give their children positive verbal reinforcement.

Parents should:

1. Read the introductory summary on MORAL COURAGE and discuss what a good definition would consist of for this fundamental value. This value is the combination of two powerful elements: moral values and being courageous. One alone will not completely work. Moral values have to be implemented. Together, these two elements form a mighty alliance. Being morally courageous can be very difficult as it demands action, forcing you outside your comfort zone. Children need to mention the action component in their definitions.

2. Parent to Child Dialogue (positive verbal reinforcement):

✓ "Stand up for what you believe."

✓ "Don't give in to pressure."

✓ "Do what you know is right."

✓ "Don't compromise yourself."

✓ "Meet your own standards, not someone else's."

✓ "Don't surrender your values!"

✓ "It may not be popular, but it's the right call."

3. Discuss the two recurring themes—the continuing presence of racial discrimination in America, and a persistent belief in the American dream of racial equality and freedom for all. Dr. King's dream was gaining freedom through moral courage despite the cost or sacrifice.

"Let freedom ring" is at the heart of the American character.

Despite Dr. King's assassination in 1968, the spirit of his moral courage is manifest in the American Civil Rights movement that continues today. Racial equality is an essential part of the American Dream that envisioned Dr. King's dream would someday come true. Parents and children should discuss how their thoughts and actions can make a difference in overcoming racial prejudice and injustice. Moral courage must embrace tolerance and understanding.

MORAL COURAGE

Knowing right from wrong is important, but acting in support of what is right involves showing your moral courage. Moral judgments involve an assessment of your ethical values, while courage is being brave in showing those values. Put these two elements together and you have the ingredients for a virtuous life. Moral courage always carries a price but it is one that you must be willing to pay. It's the best family and life investment that you can make. Parents have to be willing to lead the way, coaching their children in moral courage. This is a prime example of "walking the talk," which is the greatest impact on young kids developing their own behaviors.

You can have many strengths and skills as a parent but what raises these talents to a higher level is being able to demonstrate moral courage. Just one act of moral courage by a parent can send a message that a child will not soon forget. A family devoid of moral courage is empty. A family with moral courage is alive and vibrant in its moral tone and conditioning. Parents standing firm for great values and fighting for these values will be admired by their kids.

❖ To have courage is superior, but to have moral courage is supremacy. Character parenting sustained and guided by high moral principles is all powerful.

HOLD YOUR MORAL HIGH GROUND!

> As a character coach, do not just talk about your moral courage, demonstrate it in your daily actions. Walk your moral talk.
>
> *Coaching Tip*

MORAL COURAGE—"I Have a Dream" (1963)
Dr. Martin Luther King, Jr.

Dr. Martin Luther King (1929–1968) was a major American civil rights leader and winner of the Noble Peace Prize. Dr. King was a believer in nonviolent social action that strived to bring racial equality throughout the United States. The "I Have a Dream" speech is read at gatherings that honor Dr. King's birthday, January 15, now recognized as a national holiday. In 1963, Dr. King delivered his famous speech standing in front of the Lincoln Memorial in Washington, D.C.

MORAL COURAGE—Questions:
1. Who was Martin Luther King, Jr.?

2. Has Dr. King's call for freedom and racial equality been answered?

3. When you know someone is being treated wrong by others, do you have the courage to speak up?

4. How can Dr. King's dreams best be summarized?

5. What can we all do to help realize the hopes and dreams expressed by Dr. King?

PROFILE IN COURAGE ACTIVITY

> Teach your children that their moral courage is a special badge that they must wear daily. Tell your children to overcome their fears and let their moral courage shine through!
>
> ***Coaching Tip***

Children should:

- Develop a list of adjectives that describe a hero.
- Answer the question: "What is the difference between being courageous and morally courageous?
- Complete a "Profile in Courage" for a person who has been morally courageous.

❖ **Teach your kids about heroes, courage, and moral courage. Help them complete a Profile in Courage.**

1. **Parents will help their children do research using a dictionary and thesaurus involving the word hero.** Compile a list of twenty adjectives that describe a hero. Hero is a noun that carries many positive connotations. We all tend to look up to heroes and seemingly need them in our lives. However, finding someone who meets all the criteria to qualify as a hero is difficult. Considering the adjectives for hero, it is clear that being a hero does set some tough expectations. Discuss the hero adjectives with your children and ask them how challenging it is to meet all of these conditions. Also discuss what everyone thinks about the list of "heroes" below:

1) John Wooden

2) Martin Luther King, Jr.

3) Colin Powell

4) John F. Kennedy

5) Mother Teresa

6) Ronald Reagan

7) Abraham Lincoln

8) Amelia Earhart

9) Helen Keller

10) Caesar Chavez

You may have to do a little research to identify everyone in the list. How do your hero adjectives apply to the above list? Can you think of other people you feel would qualify as heroes? Family and friends can also qualify as heroes. You can be a hero!

2. Discuss with your children the difference between being courageous and morally courageous. Explain how it is good to be brave, but

showing your courage for principles and beliefs focuses your ability to be a person of character. Discuss how being morally courageous allows you to display the full range of your character values. Your daily actions should reveal that you are not shy about showing your character. Let your true self shine through!

3. Assist your child in writing a Profile in Courage. Consider the statements listed on the "A PROFILE IN COURAGE" sheet as requirements for whoever you select. Your profile person should demonstrate these qualities. Children can select someone famous, a person they know, a friend or family member. The profile needs to include:

- Name of person
- Explanation of how this person showed their moral courage.
- Why are you impressed by this?
- What lesson does this act of moral courage teach us?

A PROFILE IN COURAGE

TAKING RISKS

A HIGHER CALLING

GRACE UNDER PRESSURE

BEYOND THE CALL OF DUTY

CHAMPION OF A GOOD CAUSE

12. Lesson on TRUTH

> For others to believe in you, always tell them the truth.
>
> *Coaching Tip*

TRUTH Lesson Objectives:
- Children will write a definition of TRUTH.
- Parents will give their children positive verbal reinforcement.

Parents should:
1. Read the introductory summary on TRUTH and discuss a good definition for this formidable value. The problem with this value is that there are many consequences in not telling the truth. Being completely open and honest about everything is easier said than done. Sometimes we don't tell people exactly how we feel because we are being polite or tactful. The telling of "white lies" or softening the truth by slanting it in your favor is done because it is easier to do and seemingly little harm is done. However, developing a habit of modifying the truth for personal advantage or benefit will in the end undermine your integrity and cause others to doubt you. To lose the trust of others is very damaging, and to repair this trust is a long and painful process.

2. Parent to Child Dialogue (positive verbal reinforcement):

✓ "Tell the truth."

✓ "Are you telling me the truth?"

✓ "Do the right thing, even when others are urging you do otherwise."

✓ "Thank you for telling me the truth."

✓ "Tell the truth and nothing but the truth."

✓ "In this family, speaking the truth is the only way."

✓ "Don't lie, cheat, or steal to get what you want."

3. Discuss how difficult it can be to determine or get at the whole truth. Sometimes we see or believe only what we want to, without considering the entire picture. A cause of this is most likely to protect and promote our own interests. Often, the truth hurts so much that we soften or alter it to stay within our comfort zone. A truth seeker is someone who boldly confronts the truth and deals with it openly and honestly. He or she will pay the price to bare the full weight of being honest, and will put integrity before self-interest.

> Train your kids in being truth seekers. Integrity is the backbone of the family.
>
> *Coaching Tip*

TRUTH

Truth, by definition, is supposed to conform to the facts and exhibit actuality. It is supposed to mirror reality and be accepted as being true. The trouble with truth is that everyone makes their own interpretations and conclusions about it. Some blend fact and fiction together without hesitation. People tend to put themselves in the best possible light and in doing so, the occasional telling of half-truths or "white lies" are viewed as acceptable. Some are comfortable with the truth in good times but will modify it during bad times. This twisting of the truth to gain advantage is commonplace in today's world, where the ends seem to justify the means.

As a parent, it is essential to tell your kids the truth. The practice of telling the truth must be consistently modeled so children will incorporate integrity into their lifestyles. A family stands on the firm ground of truth and honesty. Letting "tiny" lies into the family will ultimately lead to "great" divisions between members. Accepting a pattern of lies can, and will, escalate into major issues of trust where the line between truth and deception becomes blurred. To be faithful to the family is to be truthful. Character parenting is truthful parenting.

❖ **Staying on the pathway of truth is not always easy, but straying from it intentionally will bring pain and hardship. It is better to wrap yourself in the integrity of truth than to have it pulled out from under you.**

NEVER COMPROMISE WHAT YOU KNOW IS THE TRUTH

> Parents, tell your kids that being truthful is their responsibility. Always believing what they say is your expectation.
>
> *Coaching Tip*

TRUTH—"The Blind Men and the Elephant"
John Godfrey Saxe
Lesson 96, *McGuffey's Fifth Eclectic Reader*

THE BLIND MEN AND THE ELEPHANT

1. It was six men of Indostan,
To learning much inclined,
Who went to see the elephant,
(Though all of them were blind,)
That each by observation
Might satisfy his mind.

2. The first approached the elephant,
And, happening to fall

Against his broad and sturdy side,
At once began to bawl:
"God bless me! but the elephant
Is very like a wall!"

3. The second, feeling of the tusk,
Cried: "Ho! What have we here,
So very round, and smooth, and sharp?
To me 't is very clear,
This wonder of an elephant
Is very like a spear!"

4. The third approached the animal,
And, happening to take
The squirming trunk within his hands,
Thus boldly up he spoke:
"I see," quoth he, "the elephant
Is very like a snake!"

5. The fourth reached out his eager hand,
And fell about the knee:
"What most this wondrous beast is like,
Is very plain," quoth he;
"'Tis clear enough the elephant
Is very like a tree!"

6. The fifth, who chanced to touch an ear,
Said: "E'en the blindest man
Can tell what this resembles most:
Deny the fact who can,
This marvel of an elephant
Is very like a fan!"

7. The sixth no sooner had begun
About the beast to grope,
Than, seizing on the swinging tail
That fell within his scope,
"I see," quoth he, "the elephant
Is very like a rope!"

8. And so these men of Indostan
Disputed long and long,
Each in his own opinion
Exceeding stiff and strong,
Though each was partly in the right,
And they were in the wrong!

TRUTH—Questions:

1. Why did each of the men from Indostan think they were right?

2. What could they have done to figure out what the elephant really looked like?

3. Do you think people sometimes act "blind" when seeking the truth?

4. How can people better understand what is really true?

5. Are you a "truth seeker" who persists until you have the whole truth?

FIVE QUESTIONS ACTIVITY

Parents, tell your kids to be truthful in what they think and do. Truthfulness must be an automatic response!

Coaching Tip

Children should:

- Read and discuss the FIVE QUESTIONS with their parents.
- Explain which of the FIVE QUESTIONS is the most difficult to follow.
- Design a poster illustrating the FIVE QUESTIONS.

❖ **Coach your children through the FIVE QUESTIONS. Realize that these are the benchmarks of integrity and help them design a poster illustrating them.**

1. **Parents should read and discuss the FIVE QUESTIONS with their children.** Truth is the supreme test of our lives. Convenience and temporary advantage are some rationale that people use to justify their actions in ignoring or concealing the truth. Some people become "truth evaders" because they have fallen into the habit of twisting the facts and have come to believe that this is actually "right." This habit must be broken. Some feel that they have the right to "manage" the truth because their end goals completely justify their actions. This is the classic "ends justify the means" strategy used by so many. The basic recommended family strategy is to implement the FIVE QUESTIONS rule when in search of the truth.

2. **Considering the FIVE QUESTIONS, which one do you feel is the most difficult one to follow?** Why is it hard to do? TRUSTWORTHINESS is a quality at the heart of a Championship Family. If family members cannot openly trust one another, little can truly be won and certainly championships will never be gained. Learning to tell the truth and build mutual trust is critically important to the health and welfare of individuals and the family.

3. **Using the FIVE QUESTIONS, help your children design a colorful 8 × 10 poster that includes responses to all of the questions.** Emphasize to your children that the answers to these questions will forever define them as a person of character and integrity. Both the question and response should be part of the poster. Use vivid colors, pictures and graphics to liven up the poster. When finished, display or hang poster in a prominent place. Hopefully, you will look at it often and remember your responses.

FIVE QUESTIONS

Family members must pledge themselves to be truth seekers and open with one another. This means always telling the truth, keeping promises and honoring your family through honesty.

I. ARE YOU A TRUSTWORTHY PERSON?

II. DO YOU ALWAYS IDENTIFY THE TRUTH?

III. CAN YOU ALWAYS BE COUNTED ON TO TELL THE TRUTH?

IV. ARE YOU A PERSON OF INTEGRITY (FAIR AND HONEST)?

V. DO YOU ACTIVELY USE THE TRUTH TO BUILD UNDERSTANDING AND FRIENDSHIPS?

JOURNAL: LIFESTYLE

A Championship Family needs to appreciate that every member has a variety of interests and talents. Family members need to fully participate in life and laugh together. A family needs to immerse itself in an active lifestyle performing like the champions they are!

FAMILY **HOBBIES**

FAMILY **SPORTS**

FAMILY **COOKBOOK**

FAMILY **HUMOR**

FAMILY **BEST TIMES**

FAMILY HOBBIES

Journal Assignment: All family members will select a new or continue a previous hobby. Everyone will prepare a short talk on what they would like to accomplish with their hobby over the month. These "hobby talks" can be given during a time when the family is together. See format for "MY HOBBY" talks.

Anything that a person likes to do can be considered a hobby. Typical kinds of hobbies are collectibles, do-it-yourself and arts activities. Some people collect stamps or baseball cards, others do woodworking or quilting, and others like to draw or play a musical instrument. Hobbies can even become a career for people. Above all else, hobbies should be fun to do.

Hobbies offer enjoyment, satisfaction, learning experiences, relaxation, opportunities for friendships and can even lead to financial profit. Hobbies are a healthy lifestyle that needs to be encouraged for everyone in the family.

- ☐ Ten Popular COLLECTION HOBBIES: ANTIQUES, BOOKS, COINS, DOLLS, MINIATURES, PHOTOGRAPHS, SPORTS CARDS, SPORTS MEMORABILIA, STAMPS, OLD TOOLS.
- ☐ Ten Popular DO-IT-YOURSELF ACTIVITIES: BAKING, BASKET WEAVING, CARVING, GARDENING, HOME IMPROVEMENT, MODELING, QUILTING, SCRAPBOOKING, SEWING, WOOD-WORKING.
- ☐ Ten Popular ARTS ACTIVITIES: DANCING, DRAMA, DRAWING, JEWELRY MAKING, PLAYING MUSICAL INSTRUMENTS, PAINTING, POETRY, SCULPTURE, WRITING.

MY HOBBY

☐ MY FAVORITE HOBBY IS ______________________________

DESCRIBE WHAT YOU DO OR WOULD LIKE TO DO WITH YOUR HOBBY AND WHY YOU LIKE IT SO MUCH.

Include a hobby action photo

FAMILY SPORTS

Journal Assignment: All family members will talk about a sport that they do or would like to do. This can even be a sport that they enjoy watching and following.

Anything that a person likes to do athletically can be included, as well as sports they enjoy watching and following. Sports activities are grouped as either individual or done in groups or teams. Sports can lead to activities that are good for fitness and socializing with friends.

Sports offer opportunities for exercise, enjoyment, friendships, learning experiences, relaxation and fun. Sports are a healthy outlet and lifestyle for Championship Families.

☐ Some Popular SPORTS ACTIVITIES:

ARCHERY	BADMINTON
BASEBALL	BASKETBALL
BILLIARDS & POOL	BOWLING
DANCING	FISHING
FOOTBALL	GOLF
HIKING	MINIATURE GOLF
RUNNING	SNOWBOARDING
SOCCER	SOFTBALL
SKIING (SNOW & WATER)	SKATEBOARDING
SKATING (ROLLER BLADE & ICE)	SURFING
SWIMMING	TENNIS
VOLLEYBALL	WALKING

MY SPORT

☐ MY FAVORITE SPORT IS ______________________________

DESCRIBE WHAT YOU DO OR WOULD LIKE TO DO WITH YOUR SPORT AND WHY YOU LIKE IT SO MUCH.

Include a sports action photo

FAMILY COOKBOOK

Journal Assignment: All family members will help put together a cookbook. Everyone will contribute their own favorite recipes for at least three or more of the ten cookbook categories. Recipes can come from any source, such as cookbooks, magazines, Internet, friends, or from anyone. Recipes can be original or borrowed. Use the FAMILY RECIPE FORMAT.

Family food recipes can be very special, including those handed down from earlier generations. Collecting and achieving family recipes on 3 × 5 index cards should be an on-going practice. Memories of good meals last a lifetime!

To identify each recipe, the contributor's first name and original recipe title need to be used. For example: "Michael's Incredible Pizza" or "Joann's Sensational Pasta Salad." Preparation steps should be clearly written to include the necessary ingredients and recommended amounts. Once all of the family recipes have been submitted, special breakfasts, lunches and dinners need to be scheduled to include them. Parents will assist their kids in their recipe preparations as needed, and kids can help their parents as they prepare theirs.

The TEN FAMILY COOKBOOK CATEGORIES:

- BREAKFAST
- SANDWICHES
- SOUPS
- SALADS
- MAIN DISHES
- PASTA DISHES
- VEGETABLE DISHES
- HEALTHY SNACKS
- COOKIES
- SMOOTHIES

Recipe cards need to be kept in a file box labeled "FAMILY COOKBOOK RECIPES" located in the kitchen for ready reference and use.

FAMILY RECIPE FORMAT

RECIPE TITLE: **Tommie's Tasty Six Bean Salad**

COMMENTS: This is an expanded version of the traditional Three Bean salad recipe. Prepare yourself for a "tasty" dynamic bean treat.

PREPARATION:

1. *Drain:* *1 can green beans*
   1 can wax beans
2. *Rinse in strainer & drain:*
   1 can garbanzo beans
   1 can black beans
   1 can pinto beans
   1 can kidney beans
3. *Mix:* *11⁄42 cup apple cider vinegar*
   11⁄42 cup sugar
   11⁄42 cup canola oil
4. *Combine all ingredients in a plastic bowl with a snug fitting lid. Store in refrigerator for a minimum of 24 hours before serving. (Tip container down and right a few times to mix ingredients during the 24 hour period. Make sure that lid is securely fastened prior to tipping.)*

Journal Assignment: Every family member will contribute one or more humorous stories or funny jokes to be included in the FAMILY JOURNAL. Humor is the catalyst of good times where people laugh and enjoy themselves. A Championship Family makes itself heard around the block with laughter. A daily dose of good humor and laughter is essential to good health and resiliency. Always be on the lookout for good jokes and humor that are present as each day unfolds itself.

However, humor that causes others to be embarrassed or relies on vulgarity is banned in the Championship Family. There is no substitute for good, clean humor.

A family that enjoys life enjoys humor and laughter to the fullest measure. Humor can help cut through the tensions and challenges everyone has. As they occur, funny family stories and comments made by every family member, including toddlers, needs to be written down. Keep a notebook handy just for the purpose of writing down funny comments or situations. These all can be added to your own family humor.

Humor can come from a variety of commercial sources as well as from family living. The important thing is to be on the outlook for the outrageous and the sublime. Remember that life is a strange mixture of the profound and the ridiculous, and movement between the two can occur in an instant.

Types of humor:

WIT—Humor that comes across as "intellectual," which is very quick and perceptive. Usually hits with a rapid fire one liner.

SATIRE—Humor that plays on the abundant weakness and identifying habits we all have. It's okay to laugh at yourself, everybody else does!

SARCASM—Humor that is biting, generally seen as putting people or events down with comic effect. A tiny bit goes a L-O-N-G way!

IRONY—Humor that may start as a compliment but swiftly changes gears to gently "sting" the unwary. Tone of voice can do the "damage."

FARCE/SLAPSTICK—Humor based on outlandish, silly situations and behavior. It's fun to get wild sometimes.

MIMICRY—Humor that pokes fun at people by imitating their gestures and speech. Watch how you talk or gesture, because you might hear or see it again! Ouch!

Murphy's Law

- **Murphy's Law:** *If anything can go wrong, it will and at the worst possible moment.*
- **Murphy's Second Law:** *Everything takes longer than you expect.*
- **Murphy's Third Law:** *Nothing is as simple as it looks.*
- "Even Championship Families cannot escape Murphy's Laws or Newton's Laws! What goes up usually comes down in unexpected places and at the worst possible time!"

FAMILY BEST TIMES

Journal Assignment: All family members submit their entry for a "family best times." Any great activity or event that the family experiences together can be written up. To qualify for a "best times" consider all the fun and exciting things that the family does together. If for any reason you can't think of a particular event or episode, think of something the family could do together for fun and suggest it happen!

Good times together are the "heartland" of family life. Strive to make them happen often. Get the family on the go when you can!

Some suggestions:

AMUSEMENT PARK

ZOO

BEACH, MOUNTAIN, LAKE, DESERT DAY

SPORTS OUTING

MOVIE

LIVE THEATER

MUSICAL CONCERT

WALKING THROUGH THE NEIGHBORHOOD

EATING OUT AT A FANCY RESTAURANT

MUSEUM TRIP

TRIP TO GRANDPARENTS

TRAIN TRIP

BOAT EXCURSION

PICNIC IN THE PARK

LIBRARY DAY

BOOKSTORE RAID

VISIT HISTORICAL PLACE

MOVIE MARATHON AT HOME

SUNDAY DRIVE

GETTING WITH FRIENDS

GOING TO CHURCH EVENT

TOURING MODEL HOMES

BBQ

MY BEST TIME

☐ A FAVORITE TIME WAS ______________________________

DESCRIBE WHAT YOU DID AND EXPLAIN WHY YOU ENJOYED IT SO MUCH.

Include a best times action photo

CHAPTER THREE

PRACTICE SESSIONS: (Learning Out

For family members to show their CHARACTER they need t
tice some key values. PRACTICE SESSIONS will help prepare
ilies for life's fierce and relentless competitions. To be competi
children need to become proficient with their skills in COMMUI
CATION, CONFIDENCE, JUDGMENT, KNOWLEDGE and
RESPONSIBILITY. Both parents and their children can each increase their skill levels in these Learning Outcome Values. PRACTICE SESSIONS is where the family can:

- Achieve a series of important LEARNING OUTCOMES.
- Develop an awareness of the extensive role of **COMMUNICATION.**
- Learn the all-powerful importance of **CONFIDENCE.**
- Make some tough **JUDGMENT** calls that will occur throughout life.
- Realize the immense power of **KNOWLEDGE.**
- Accept **RESPONSIBILITY** without conditions.

> Parents, guide your children by helping them practice and get ready for life's tests. Coach and teach them well so they will be ready to sustain their character values. How does a child value character? Practice makes all the difference! Coach and teach them well so they can listen before speaking, believe in themselves, consider the consequences, grasp the awesome power of knowledge, and make no excuses for themselves.
>
> *Coaching Tip*

n COMMUNICATION

> u, when they know you are
>
> *Coaching Tip*

ION Lesson Objectives:

will write a definition of COMMUNICATION.

s will give their children positive verbal reinforcement.

Parents should

1. Read the introductory summary of COMMUNICATION and discuss with your children the basic language skills (listening, speaking, reading and writing) and how each one is challenging. Assist your child with their writing a clear and concise definition of this all important skill. Ask them which language skill is their strongest point. Which ones do they feel they need to strengthen? Which one do they feel is the most important? Why? In what ways can a family benefit from practices of good communication skills between family members? A full definition should stress the many benefits of this extensive skill.

2. Parent to Child Dialogue (positive verbal reinforcement):

✓ "I hear what you are saying."

✓ "I am listening to you."

✓ "In other words, this is what you mean?"

✓ "You've made an excellent point."

✓ "Could you explain what you mean?"

✓ "Your reading comprehension is excellent."

✓ "This is a very well written paper, good job!"

3. Explain why a few, well chosen words can be more effective in communicating an idea than several pages of rambling thoughts

Discuss the causes and outcomes of the **American Civil War** that was fought from 1861 to 1865. Americans fought Americans over issues of slavery, politics and sectional differences. The battle of Gettysburg (July 1–3, 1863) is considered a major turning point of the Civil War as the Union defeated the Confederate army in its attempt to invade Pennsylvania. The overwhelming advantages of population and industrial strength of the North would ensure the eventual defeat of the South. Explain to your children how the Civil War greatly changed the United States by strengthening the Constitution as the supreme law of the land. Also discuss the key role played by Abraham Lincoln, considered by many to be America's greatest President.

COMMUNICATION

The act of communication is the understanding of words and messages between two or more people. It is our greatest single strength and ironically, our most fundamental weakness. Communication, both spoken and written, is the reason for our successes and the advancement of civilization. However, failure to effectively communicate has caused recurring misunderstandings and disagreements between people, which have lead to arguments and even warfare. The language skills of listening, speaking, reading and writing are an integral part of the operation of any family. At times, these communication skills can falter and break down in the home. A family is always at risk of experiencing communication gaps and failures, including a refusal to listen to each other that results in dysfunction and "guerilla warfare."

Parents need to be great communicators. Parents must connect and fully communicate with their children. Eye contact and a sincere desire to really hear what is being said by family members are essential when practicing communication skills. Thoughtful words and meaningful dialogue, like maximum use of positive verbal reinforcement, are the ingredients of good communication. Listen carefully to what others are saying and then think about what your response will be. Don't prepare your response before you hear what the other person is saying. We often think about what we are going to say while the other person is talking. This action blocks communication. **Communication should always be used for motivation, reinforcement and understanding.**

❖ **Never underestimate the virtue of good communication skills. Be concise and clear in your message.**

LISTEN BEFORE SPEAKING

> **LISTEN—actively**
> **SPEAK—persuasively**
> **READ—enthusiastically**
> **WRITE—passionately**
> These are the actions of a great communicator.
>
> *Coaching Tip*

COMMUNICATION—GETTYSBURG ADDRESS (1863)
Abraham Lincoln

GETTYSBURG ADDRESS

"Four score and seven years ago our fathers brought forth on this continent, a new nation, conceived in liberty, and dedicated to the proposition that all men are created equal.

Now we are engaged in a great civil war, testing whether that nation, or any nation so conceived and so dedicated, can long endure. We are met on a great battlefield of that war. We have come to dedicate a portion of that field, as a final resting place for those who here gave their lives that a nation might live. It is altogether fitting and proper that we should do this.

But, in a larger sense, we can not dedicate—we can not consecrate—we can not hallow—this ground. The brave men, living and dead, who struggled here, have consecrated it, far above our poor power to add or detract. The world will little note, not long remember what we say here. It is for us the living, rather, to be dedicated here to the unfinished work which they have thus far so nobly advanced. It is rather for us to be here dedicated to the great task remaining before us—that from these honored dead we take increased devotion to that cause for which they gave their last full measure—that we here highly resolve that these dead men shall not have died in vain—that this great nation, under God, shall have a new birth of freedom—and that the government of the people, by the people, for the people, shall not perish from the earth."

COMMUNICATION—Questions:

1. Who was Abraham Lincoln?

2. What happened at the Battle of Gettysburg in 1863?

3. Why do you think that the Gettysburg Address is considered to be such a great speech?

4. What do you think is the central message of the Gettysburg Address?

5. Edward Everett, the principal speaker at the Gettysburg dedication later wrote to Lincoln, "I should be glad if I could flatter myself that I came as near to the central idea of the occasion in two hours as you did in two minutes." What is the advantage and great challenge of a short speech over long ones?

FAMILY NEWSLETTER ACTIVITY

> A family must wrap their communications with each other in understanding, positive thoughts, and love.
>
> *Coaching Tip*

Children should:

- Understand the 5W's of reporting (Who, What, When, Where, Why).
- Practice the three steps of writing: *composing, reading*, and *rewriting*.
- Participate with parents in writing a monthly newsletter.

❖ **ASSIGNMENT: Children practice the basics of writing and reporting as the family publishes their own newsletter.**

1. **Using newspaper and magazine articles, children will identify the 5 W's.** Kids will select an article illustrating examples of:

- Who was involved and mentioned in the article?
- What took place, describe the circumstances and explain the events?
- When did the events described take place?

- Where did the events described take place?

- Why did the events take place? (This may or may not be explained.)

Parents will discuss this exercise with their kids and point out the difference between **fact** and **opinion**. Also discuss how any photos, graphics, diagrams or maps were used in the articles. How do these special features enhance the overall understanding of the articles?

2. **Children will write a short paragraph on any recent or memorable family event.** Parents will guide their kids through the three basic steps of writing:

Step One—COMPOSING: Getting started is perhaps the toughest part but encourage your kids to settle on a story and start putting their thoughts and ideas on paper as quickly as possible. Kids shouldn't worry about spelling and grammar, just put down some ideas. They need to let their ideas and memories flow freely onto the paper. Parents will point out how a paragraph usually includes a topic sentence containing the main idea and how the other sentences are used to explain and amplify the central thought.

Step Two—READING: Kids will read their paragraphs to each other and to their parents. Does the story explain everything and does it make sense? Does anything need further explanation? Is the story understandable? Should anything be deleted or added?

Step Three—REWRITING: Everyone needs to appreciate the need for rewriting stories. Now is the time to check for grammar and spelling. With help from their parents, kids should rewrite their paragraphs. Good paragraphs are the direct result of good sentences. There are two important suggestions for young writers to bear in mind. First, write in the present tense, "Our family drove to the beach for the day." Second, use the first person and include how you feel, "I always get excited about going to the beach with the family."

3. **Family members will put together a family newsletter.** Parents will act as newsletter editors having the final say in what is and what is not included in this family publication. Every family member is a reporter and they are required to submit at least one article for each edition. The editors may ask the kids on their reporting staff for rewrites and can help them in this process. Newsletter preparation will involve:

Newsletter Logo and Heading
Family logos can be practically anything from a graphic design or picture. Even a reduced copy of the family crest could be used for this purpose. Newsletter headings or titles could be something catchy, such as *AMAZING ANNALS, TERRIFIC TIMES, SPECIAL ISSUE, BREAKING NEWS, FOR YOUR EYES ONLY* or *FAMILY REPORTER.*

Newsletter Features
Editors will make newsletter assignments but reporters can always volunteer to do various sections.

- ☐ Feature Stories: These are major family stories that can include photos. Title of story will be followed by a byline listing the reporter. Newsletter can include one or two feature stories. Story titles can include a little mystery or humor to them such as, *UFO's Spotted Hovering above House* or *Family Survives Weekend.*

- ☐ Family Interviews: Reporters can interview both family and friends. The interview can include focus questions such as:
  "What would you like to change about anything?"
  "If you suddenly won a million dollars, what would you do?"
  "If you could travel to any place, where would you go and why?"
  "Would you be willing to go to Mars? Why or why not?"

- ☐ Question & Answer of the Month: Family members should be encouraged to submit questions. Editors will determine who should answer these questions. Questions can be anonymous.

- ☐ Entertainment Review: This could be a movie, video, CD or television show. Reporter should explain why they thought it was good or bad and give it a rating with five stars being best.

- ☐ Quotes of the Month: The quotes can be actual, made up, or from any source as long as they somehow relate to the family. Even the pets can be quoted as long as they give their permission.

Newsletter Preparation

Editors will conduct the final assembly of the newsletter. Newsletters can be put together using desktop publishing or by cutting and pasting. They can also be photocopied on colored paper. One copy should be placed in the FAMLY JOURNAL. Each family member will be given a copy of the newsletter at a time when everyone will be able to read and enjoy it together.

> Fond memories and good times are the result of both spontaneous and planned activities, which are the essence of Championship Families.
>
> *Coaching Tip*

Family Chronicle

MONTHLY NEWSLETTER OF THE SMITH FAMILY

Number XX Month of APRIL

SMITH'S HOLD ANNUAL GARAGE SALE by JANE SMITH

FAMILY INTERVIEW: RICKY SMITH by ALAN SMITH

TOUGH QUESTIONS & GREAT ANSWERS
by RICKY SMITH

ENTERTAINMENT REVIEW OF THE TOP FIVE MOVIES
by MARY SMITH

QUOTES FOR APRIL

"Be ready to fill empty spaces of your day with positive thoughts about someone in this family."—MS

"Knock before entering!"—RS

"Lost: A little time. Found: Much love."—JS

"The greatest prize? All of you!"—AS

14. Lesson on **CONFIDENCE**

> Take a moment and say to everyone in the family, "I believe in you."
>
> *Coaching Tip*

CONFIDENCE Lesson Objectives:

- Children will write a definition of CONFIDENCE.
- Parents will give their children positive verbal reinforcement.

Parents should:

1. Read the summary of CONFIDENCE. Tell your children how much you believe in them. The importance of having confidence throughout life is vital to all family members. A Championship Family is a confident family. Every member is confident in their relationships and know they are supported and believed in by others. Explain the difference between being confident and arrogant. To be overly prideful is counter to presenting yourself openly and honestly. Confidence is a genuine and sincere feeling. Self-assurance comes from being loved and respected within a family.

2. Parent to Child Dialogue (positive verbal reinforcement):

✓ "I believe in you."

✓ "I have always believed in you."

✓ "I will always believe in you."

✓ "I know you have what it takes."

✓ "You have a lot of things going for you."

✓ "Everyone in the family believes in you."

✓ "We believe in you."

President Reagan's inspirational words were meant to call a nation to action at home and abroad. When Reagan took "inventory," he was putting together a national resume based on a nation of freedom, composed of countless American heroes. This address called Americans to believe in themselves again and to go forth and do great things. Reagan was telling Americans that they needed to actively believe in themselves and in their abilities to pursue greatness. This is what parent coaches need to constantly do with their children—to summon them to greatness and to reinforce them as capable people. Never stop believing in your children.

CONFIDENCE

Self-assurance is a combination of experiences and positive attitudes resulting from being successful with people and situations. Confidence and success are tightly intertwined. Parents are chief agents in helping to build the confidence of their children. The more nurturing that a child receives from their parents, the higher their self-confidence will soar. It all starts with parents establishing a strong foundation of confidence by being their children's principal advocates and champions. If at first you truly believe in your child, they have the greatest chance at believing in themselves.

Being certain about yourself and your abilities sets the stage for great things to happen. Parents that spend time to build their children's confidence will see them grow as positive family members, good students and successful adults. Confident students and adults became that way because they had parents as cheerleaders. This sets in motion an expectation of mutual encouragement in the family and with friends. Confident kids seek out confident friends and positive relationships. Once ignited, the flame of confidence will burn brightly in the lives of all who grasp this quality and never let it go.

❖ **Self-confidence is critically important to growing as a person. Believing in yourself helps you take risks and accept momentary failure. Confidence will keep you in the game even when the going gets tough.**

BELIEVE IN YOURSELF

> Parents, build the confidence of your children with positive words and supportive actions.
>
> *Coaching Tip*

CONFIDENCE—FIRST INAUGURAL ADDRESS
of RONALD REAGAN (Excerpt from Speech)
January 20, 1981

As for the enemies of freedom, those who are potential adversaries, they will be reminded that peace is the highest aspiration of the American people. We will negotiate for it, sacrifice for it; we will not surrender for it—now or ever.

Directly in front of me, the monument to a monumental man: George Washington, Father of Our Country. A man of humility who came to greatness reluctantly. He led America out of revolutionary victory into infant nationhood. Off to one side , the stately memorial to Thomas Jefferson. The Declaration of Independence fames with his eloquence.

And then beyond the Reflecting Pool the dignified columns of the Lincoln Memorial. Whoever would understand in his heart the meaning of America will find it in the life of Abraham Lincoln.

Beyond those monuments to heroism is the Potomac River, and on the far shore the sloping hills of Arlington National Cemetery with row upon row of simple white markers bearing crosses or stars of David. They add up to only a tiny fraction of the price that has been paid for our freedom.

Under one marker lies a young man – Martin Treptow – who left his job in a small town barber shop in 1917 to go to France with the famed Rainbow Division. There, on the western front, he was killed trying to carry a message between battalions under heavy artillery fire.

We are told that on his body was found a diary. On the flyleaf under the heading, "My pledge," he had written these words: "America must win this war. Therefore, I will work, I will save, I will sacrifice, I will endure, I will fight cheerfully and do my utmost, as if the issue of the whole struggle depended on me alone."

The crisis we are facing today does not require of us the kind of sacrifice that Martin Treptow and so many thousands of others were called upon to make. It does require, however, our best effort, and our willingness to believe that together, with God's help, we can and will resolve the problems which now confront us.

CONFIDENCE—Questions:

1. Who was Ronald Reagan?

2. In his speech, who are Reagan's heroes?

3. How was President Reagan's inaugural in 1981 different from the previous ones? How was the location changed?

4. Who was Martin Treptow? How did he show his confidence?

5. Has your family ever visited Washington D.C.? (If not, a family visit to our nation's Capitol must be a high priority.)

RESUME ACTIVITY

> Every family member should periodically take stock of their objectives, values, and direction.
>
> *Coaching Tip*

Children should:

- Write a short-term personal objective as well as long-term objective.
- List their Core and Life Skill Values.
- Prepare a complete written resume.

❖ **ASSIGNMENT: Children will prepare their own background information and write a resume.**

1. **Children will write some short-term personal objectives that can be accomplished within one year and a long-term objective that can be realized in future years.**

• Short-term objectives: This is anything that can be done in less than a year. Accomplishment should be something of a significant nature, such as learning a new skill (artistic, musical or athletic), or pursuing a new hobby or interest. Whatever activity is selected, it should be something that hasn't been tried before. Tell your children that it is important to master new skills, because it will increase self-esteem, thereby increasing confidence. Another key point is that any short-term objective should not be quickly given up, but pursued with some amount of perseverance.

• Long-term objective: Again, this could literally be anything of a major category from inventing a cure for cancer to even becoming President of the United States. The sky is the limit when contemplating future accomplishments. Future occupations could also be listed, along with reasons why a future career has been chosen. A long-term objective can be changed over time, but it is fun to contemplate different future goals. Career exploration can be interesting at any age. Kids should ask their parents why they chose their careers and other long-term objectives in their lives.

> The seeds of great accomplishments can be planted early in life and watered frequently by confidence.
>
> *Coaching Tip*

2. **Children should consider and list their Core Values along with their Life Skill Values.** The five core values selected should represent those that are held closest and thought to be the most essential. Also, select five life skill values and why you feel they are important. List your values in capital letters with a short reason why they have been chosen.

- Core Values: ABILITY, CHARACTER, RESPECT, CARING, FAITH, LOVE, MORAL COURAGE, TRUTH, RESPONSIBILITY, SERVICE, TACT and VIRTUE.
- Life Skill Values: MOTIVATION, PERSEVERANCE, CREATIVITY, FITNESS, COMMUNICATION, CONFIDENCE, JUDGMENT, KNOWLEDGE, DECISION-MAKING, LEADERSHIP, ORGANIZATION and TEAMWORK.

3. **A completed RESUME:**

☐ Heading will include full name and address information. Name should be in large letters so there is no mistaking whose resume it is.

- ☐ Objectives will include both short and one long-term. Rationale for them will be brief and be kept to a sentence or two.

- ☐ Core and Life Skill Values will be listed, along with a brief explanation as to why they have been selected.

- ☐ Final statement will summarize how the objectives and values point the way to a confident and successful future. Any kid's future has to be bright when considering the great things anticipated and the holding of positive values.

Consider the suggested RESUME FORMAT when putting together resumes (see page 118). Formatting is very important when writing a resume. The purpose of a resume is to advertise a person's qualifications and background. Adults routinely use resumes to get prospective employers interested in them and hopefully be called for a job interview. Children can develop skills at putting together a resume perhaps for the very first time. The purpose of a child's resume is to showcase their hopes and dreams, along with their values which help them to grow confident.

> The resumes of young children hold the keys to their futures. Visit them often so they will help provide kids with direction.
>
> *Coaching Tip*

(RESUME FORMAT)

FIRST NAME & LAST NAME

Objectives

Short-term:

Long-term:

Values

Core Values:

1.

2.

3.

4.

5.

Life skill values:

1.

2.

3.

4.

5.

Concluding statement

Signature ______________________________ Date __________________

15. Lesson on **JUDGMENT**

> True wisdom is considering the consequences of your decisions.
>
> *Coaching Tip*

JUDGMENT Lesson Objectives:

- Children will write a definition of JUDGMENT.
- Parents will give their children positive verbal reinforcement.

Parents should:

1. Explain to their kids how making judgment calls continues throughout life. Making that right call can sometimes be very tough, but they still have to be made. Explain how you are the sum total of countless judgments, both major and minor. Judgments all add up and will reflect our courage to follow a positive and moral value framework. Judgments project who we are and where we stand. Kids have to know that making the "tough calls" may not be popular or easy, but they must reflect good judgment. Making quality judgment calls is where Championship Families stand and deliver.

2. Parent to Child Dialogue (positive verbal reinforcement):

✓ "That's correct."

✓ "You're right on."

✓ "You've made a good decision."

✓ "You thought that through, I'm proud of you."

✓ "Have you thought about the consequences?"

✓ "You did the right thing."

✓ "Awesome choice!"

3. Discuss the necessity of thinking things through. Parents need to say that while everyone wants acceptance from others, giving in to peer pressure or making popular choices can sometimes lead to bad judgments. To say "no" to potential trouble can carry the criticism of some but win the admiration of many. Through character coaching, build in your children the habit of thinking for themselves and not allowing someone else do the thinking for them. Surrendering judgment calls to others is why so many fall into an endless cycle of trouble. Having the resolve to say "no" to trouble is showing your good judgment.

> To love your child is to coach them in the art of making good judgments. To ignore your child is to open their door to making bad judgments.
>
> *Coaching Tip*

JUDGMENT

Judgment is forming an opinion and making an assessment to draw a conclusion. It is a process that is done continuously as we go through our daily tasks and routine. Some judgments are rather trivial while others are of great importance, which involve the integrity of our value system. Parental judgments impact on the entire family and largely shape its destiny. Good judgments should be fair and reflect an adherence to character values.

Parents exhibiting and coaching good judgment give their children the best chance at attaining this vital skill. You are as strong as your poorest judgment. Parents need to consider these five elements in guiding their judgments:

1. *Don't rush to judgment—be patient and thorough.*
2. *Enforce "the rules."*
3. *Consider the consequences.*
4. *Be fair.*
5. *Let your children know that you love them.*

Our reputations are earned by the judgments we make. Good judgment is usually the end product of a lot of mistakes. As we grow older, we realize how easy it is to jump to conclusions that sound judgment rests on patience and virtue.

❖ **Making good choices when faced with uncertainty and fear can be "tough,"which is why character coaching by parents is so important. Kids have to learn to dig deep within their value system to make their best judgment calls.**

CONSIDER THE CONSEQUENCES

> Character coaches must be both patient and fair with their children.
>
> *Coaching Tip*

JUDGMENT—"When to Say No"

Lesson 56, McGuffey's Third Eclectic Reader

WHEN TO SAY NO

1. Though "no" is a very little word, it is not always easy to say; and not doing so often causes trouble.
2. When we are asked to stay away from school and spend in idleness or mischief, the time which ought to be spent in study, we should at once say "No."
3. When we are urged to loiter on our way to school, and thus be late, and interrupt our teacher and the school, we should say "No." When some schoolmates wish us to whisper or play in the schoolroom, we should say "No."
4. When we have done anything wrong, and are tempted to conceal it by falsehood, we should say "No, we can not tell a lie; it is wicked and cowardly."
5. If we are asked to do anything which we know to be wrong, we should not fear to say, "No."

6. If we thus learn to say "No," we shall avoid much trouble, and always be safe.

Questions:
1. What advice is given to children regarding school?

2. How are we supposed to handle our anger?

3. Why is it difficult for some people to say "no" to trouble?

4. Is making good judgments easy?

5. Are you good at saying "no" when you know it is right thing to do?

FIVE TESTS ACTIVITY

> To develop good character in your child requires training and guidance in helping them make good judgments.
>
> ***Coaching Tip***

Children should:
- Review the "Five Tests" involved in making good judgment calls with their parents.

- Discuss how good character is closely intertwined with the ability and courage in using effective judgment skills.
- Design a chart that lists questions for each of the "Five Tests."

❖ **ASSIGNMENT: Kids will review the "Five Tests" model, discuss effective judgment skills and make a chart listing key questions in making judgments.**

1. **Parents should explain that while judgments sometimes miss the mark, asking five basic questions can help everyone to reach their best possible judgment calls.** To some, being ethical is a matter of convenience if it suits their purpose. If not, they will do whatever it takes to get what they want. These rule benders are only after the end result. Today's common rule of thumb is "do what you need to regardless of ethics but don't get caught." Parents should tell their kids that they cannot have a double standard. Children must follow one standard of making good judgments—not because it is harder, but because it is right.

The FIVE TESTS

I. GOLDEN RULE TEST:
"How would I like to be treated in this situation?
In short, treat others as you would like to be treated.

II. TRUTH TEST:
"Is it the truth?"
If it is not truthful, it cannot be said in good faith.

III. INTEGRITY TEST:
"Does my choice truly reflect my character values?"
It is all about knowing and doing what is right.

IV. ETHICS TEST:
"Is it the right thing to do?"
Action must reflect your moral values.

V. PRESS RELEASE TEST:

"Would I want to read about my judgment call in the morning paper or hear it discussed on the evening news?"

If everyone knew about your choice, would that be okay?

2. **Good character equals good judgment.** You cannot separate these two elements. Kids have to understand that if they make poor judgments, they are selling out their character. Losing integrity is weakening the core of your character and you cannot accept this. Character and judgment are linked, and if judgments are bad, then character is pulled in that direction. The answer is to let your good character values pull judgment calls in their direction.

3. **Parents should help their kids design a "Five Tests" chart to help guide them in making good moral judgments.** Parents will help their children write their own questions in response to the five test elements necessary to evaluate any moral judgment. See sample format of "The Five Tests."

The "Five Tests" chart can be used as a constant reminder of what needs to be considered when judgment calls are made. A lot is at stake and these tests give any judgment a rigorous workout. Bad calls will have a tough time surviving the tests of the GOLDEN RULE, TRUTH, INTEGRITY, ETHICS and PRESS RELEASE.

Average kids sometimes make poor choices.
Good kids are much better at making good choices.
Great kids consistently make excellent choices.
All kids are capable of being "great."

Coaching Tip

THE FIVE TESTS

My judgments will always be tested against the following questions:

1.

2.

3.

4.

5.

Signature ______________________________ Date ______________

16. Lesson on **KNOWLEDGE**

> Knowledge with character is a mighty force that is unstoppable in its relentless pursuit of truth.
>
> *Coaching Tip*

Lesson Objectives for KNOWLEDGE:

- Children will write a definition of KNOWLEDGE.
- Parents will give their children positive verbal reinforcement.

Parents should:

1. Point out how knowledge can be applied and used in many different ways, both positive and negative. The key to employing your knowledge effectively is to connect the "knowing" with the "doing" and always let your values guide you. The theory has to be applied to real life situations. Tell your kids how knowledge gives them the edge. The power of knowledge is released through the persistent habit of reading. Promote the thought that "readers are winners!"

2. Parent to Child Dialogue (positive verbal reinforcement):

✓ "Tell me what you have read."

✓ "Let me share what I have just read with you."

✓ "You have learned that very well."

✓ "Great, you figured it out."

✓ "That's excellent work."

✓ "You have learned a very important lesson."

✓ "I am very proud of you, you are a good reader."

3. Discuss how important it is to know why you are learning things and then how to use this knowledge constructively. Knowledge is a dynamic force. Lifelong learning is the gateway to unlimited knowledge. Kids need to realize that learning changes people and causes them to grow. To respect learning is to use it in positive and constructive ways. Yes, learning can be difficult and at times very demanding, but the rewards are very satisfying.

A Championship Family values knowledge and the great importance of education. The education of children must be a top priority for parents. As their children's first teachers, parents bear the primary responsibility for their education. Character parenting requires that parents send their children to school ready to learn, and work collaboratively with teachers to ensure that their children have every chance for success in school. A Championship Family knows that it must be committed to lifelong learning that involves all of its members.

KNOWLEDGE

Education in the home is the faithful transmission of knowledge and skills from parents to children. Knowledge is information which is perceived, discovered and learned. Education is continuous as new facts and situations present themselves. To live is to be learning something new all the time. Knowledge can be expressed as academic proficiencies, cultural mores, vocational and social skills as well as character education. To know is to take action and to serve others.

If a parent succeeds as their children's first teacher, they have been given the best chance for success in school and in life. The behavior and conduct of children at school is largely a reflection of the "home schooling" that has taken place. Parents cannot blame schools for failing until they have exhausted every opportunity and resource to help educate their own children. In support of knowledge and learning, every home should have a library of books offering every family member a rich offering of both reference, fiction and non-fiction books. Parents must actively support and encourage their children as dedicated learners. I think the current crisis in education has resulted from too many parents neglecting their role as first teachers.

❖ **Knowledge is achieved through hard work and dedication. Kids must have a quality education in order to perform critical thinking skills needed in today's ever changing and complex world.**

KNOWLEDGE IS AWESOME POWER!

KNOWLEDGE—"Knowledge is Power"
Lesson 56, *McGuffey's Fourth Eclectic Reader*

KNOWLEDGE IS POWER

1. "What an excellent thing is knowledge," said a sharp looking, bustling little man to one who was much older than himself. "Knowledge is an excellent thing," repeated he. "My boys know more at six and seven years old than I did at twelve. They can read all sorts of books, and talk on all sorts of subjects. The world is a great deal wiser than it used to be. Everyone knows something of everything now. Do you not think, sir, that knowledge is an excellent thing?"

2. "Why, Sir," replied the old man, looking grave, "that depends entirely upon the use to which it is applied. It may be a blessing or a curse. Knowledge is only an increase of power, and power may be a bad, as well as a good thing." "That is what I cannot understand," said the bustling little man. "How can power be a bad thing?"

3. "I will tell you," meekly replied the old man; and thus went on: "When the power of a horse is under restraint, the animal is useful in bearing burdens, drawing loads, and carrying his master; but when that power is unrestrained, the horse breaks his bridle, dashes to pieces the carriage that he draws, or throws his rider." "I see!" said the little man.

4. "When the water of a large pond is properly conducted by trenches, it renders the fields around fertile; but when it bursts through its banks, it sweeps everything before it and destroys the produce of the fields." "I see!" said the little man. "I see!"

5. "When the ship is steered aright, the sail that she hoists enables her sooner to get into port; but if steered wrong, the more sail she carries the further will she go out of her course." "I see!" said the little man. "I see clearly!"

6. "Well, then," continued the old man, "if you see these things so clearly, I hope you can see, too, that knowledge, to be a good thing, must be rightly applied. God's grace in the heart will render the knowledge to the head a blessing; but without this, it may prove to us no better than a curse." "I see! I see!" said the little man. "I see!"

KNOWLEDGE—Questions:

1. What advice did the older man give regarding the use of knowledge?

2. Does knowledge always give power? Is it always good?

3. What is the principle safeguard in using knowledge?

4. Can you think of any examples when the power of knowledge has ever been misused?

5. How are you using knowledge in your life?

FAMILY OF READERS ACTIVITY

> Start reading to and with your children in their preschool years and never stop.
>
> *Coaching Tip*

Children should:
- Learn about the "Six Plateaus of Knowledge" which comprise the levels of critical or extended thinking.
- Become involved with the "Parent's Rigorous Reading Plan."
- Participate in building a family library and then take the "Family Reading Challenge."

❖ **ASSIGNMENT: Assist your child in discovering levels of knowledge, engaging them in active reading, and after starting your family reader, have everyone take the "Family Reading Challenge."**

1. **Children will be able to list the six plateaus of knowledge.** These six basic elements are commonly known to educators as "Bloom's Taxonomy," levels of critical thinking and extended thinking. Read through the **SIX PLATEAUS OF KNOWLEDGE** with your children and have them memorize the six main categories. The knowledge level is the simple acquiring of information while the evaluation level involves the more complex application of what has been learned. Children need to realize that their success in school and life hinges upon their ability to process information efficiently at all levels of the plateau. They must become comfortable moving back and forth through all the levels. Young minds need to learn how to go forward, back up, go up and down and even move sideways.

2. **Parents need to follow a rigorous reading plan in motivating their children to read.** Readers are in control of their futures. Children who are avid readers have the high expectation of doing well at home, school, and later in life. Reading will help them become successful citizens, family members, workers and learners. Parents should not leave their child behind in the reading game.

PARENT'S RIGOROUS READING PLAN:

- **BEGIN READING WITH YOUR CHILD IMMEDIATELY!** If you don't have appropriate children's books, go get them. The younger your children are, the more you will have to read to them. You can borrow library books, buy them, order them, or download them, but don't stop providing this essential tool for them. Growing readers need a steady supply of books.

• **CONNECT YOUR CHILD TO THE HABIT OF READING!** Take your children to libraries and bookstores. Spend time with them searching through books with subjects that most interest them. Read articles, short stories and even the Sunday comics with them.

• **ENCOURAGE FAMILY READING!** Make reading a regular activity where everyone engages in periods of quiet reading together. The impact of young kids seeing their parents busy with reading will last a lifetime. Share your reading with your kids and ask them questions about what they have read. Championship Families are reading families.

• **RESEARCH GOOD CHILDREN'S LITERATURE!** Parents need to become experts on age appropriate books for their kids. It is okay for kids to have their reading preferences, but they should be exposed to challenging works including the classics. To be well read is to greatly expand your ability and capacity as a person.

• **MAKE READING A TOP PRIORITY!** When you schedule a regular family reading hour, ban all other pursuits and activities. Children need to be taught that family reading sessions are times when books get everyone's undivided attention. The electronic world is eclipsed by the simple yet powerful printed word.

3. **Children will participate in the building of a family library of good books.** Again, the bond between Championship Families and quality books is exceedingly strong. The family must make their library a priority both in time, effort and money. The creation of this library will be remembered and has the potential of dramatically changing the lives of everyone. Such a library literally has no limits or boundaries.

BUILDING THE FAMILY LIBRARY:

• **ESTABLISH A PRIMARY REFERENCE LIBRARY.** Reference books should include a children's dictionary, dictionary, thesaurus, encyclopedia set, world atlas, United States atlas, a collection of local city and state maps and any other reference materials. A computer with Internet access with the resources of various search engines can be considered valuable reference tools.

• **START A CHILDREN'S LITERATURE SECTION.** The hub of a family library with young kids are children's books that are age appropriate:

Pre-School—Babies and toddlers need to see and feel books from the beginning. This may start with cloth and board books. Reading can begin with the touching or biting of a book and hearing a parents' voice reading. Books in this area may be folk and fairy tales, nursery rhymes, Bible stories and children's poetry.

Kindergarten through 3rd Grade—Kids step up to a rich variety of both fiction and non- fiction books. Libraries and schools have recommended lists and titles of books that are good for this age level. Remember that the family library may be centrally located with "branch locations" in bedrooms or anywhere in the house.

4th through 6th Grade—Kids step up to an expanding domain of both fiction and non-fiction books. As definite interests develop, books must match these interests. Kids at this level are developing a sophistication and deeper awareness of literature that will shape their intellectual curiosity and use of reading as a major learning tool.

• **AUGMENT THE FAMILY LIBRARY.** As children grow up, so will the family library. Teenagers and adults will require age appropriate books. Parents are encouraged to expand their reading section to include those books that are of interest to them.

• **ORGANIZE THE FAMILY LIBRARY.** With the gradual accumulation of books, the family library will need to be periodically reorganized. The DEWEY DECIMAL CLASSIFICATION system can be of help to larger, more unwieldy book collections. Above all else, a family should have fun with its library and make it a focus of their time together.

THE FAMILY READING CHALLENGE

A poster board will be placed on the wall in the living or family room. In large block letters at the top of the poster board, "FAMILY READING CHALLENGE" will be written. Each time any family member completes reading an entire book, the book title and author, along with the family member's name, will be printed on the poster board. The reading goal for the family over a year will be one hundred books. This can be adjusted for larger reading families. The family member with the most books listed on the board will be honored by a special dinner and reading trophy.

SIX PLATEAUS OF KNOWLEDGE

1. **RECALL**—PERSON CALLS, RECITES, LISTS, LABELS, NAMES, REPEATS. INFORMATION IS LEARNED AND REMEMBERED.

   Example: Say or recite the Pledge of Allegiance.

2. **COMPREHENSION**—PERSON SHOWS UNDERSTANDING OF INFORMATION BY DEMONSTRATING, EXPLAINING, DECRIBING, INTERPRETING OR SUMMARIZING.

   Say in your own words what the following means: "Pledge allegiance" and "Liberty and justice for all."

3. **APPLICATION**—PERSON USES INFORMATION IN DISCUSSING AND RELATING IT TO NEW SITUATIONS AND CONDITIONS.

   How are "liberty" and "justice" exhibited?

4. **ANALYSIS**—PERSON EXAMINES SPECIFIC PARTS OF THE INFORMATION BY CLASSIFYING, CATEGORIZING AND MAKING CAUSE AND EFFECT RELATIONSHIPS.

   What parts of the Pledge of Allegiance refer to you and to the country?

5. **SYNTHESIS**—PERSON DOES SOMETHING NEW AND DIFFERENT WITH THE INFORMATION SUCH AS CREATING, DESIGNING, MODIFYING, PLANNING AND REVISING.

   Write a Championship Family pledge that all of your family would be willing to sign.

6. **EVALUATION**—PERSON JUDGES THE INFORMATION BY ASSESSING, RATING, VALUING OR SELECTING.

   Should every American say the Pledge?

THE CHAMPIONSHIP FAMILY LIBRARY

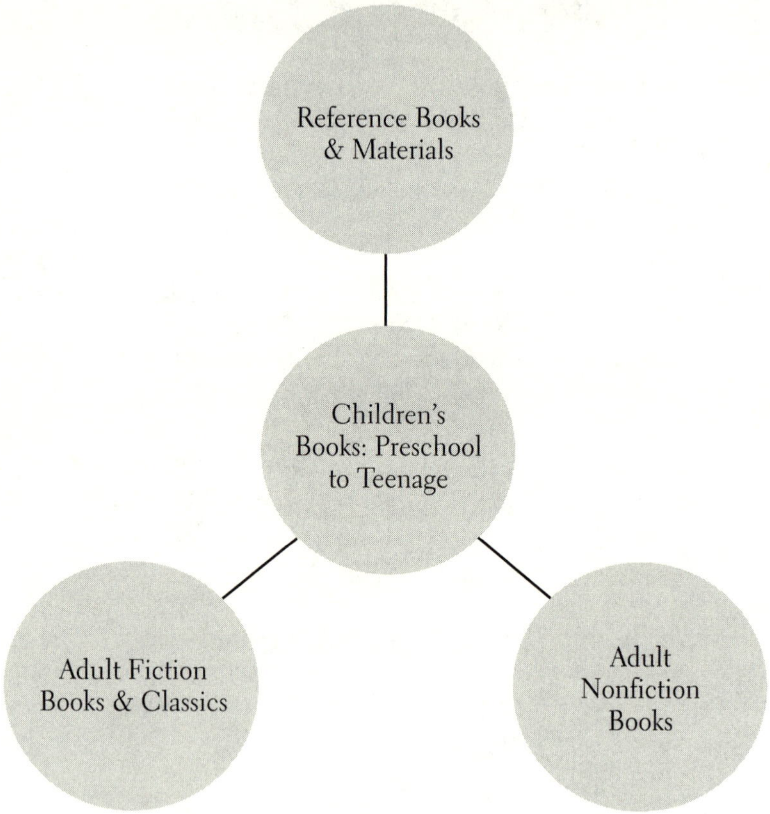

THE DEWEY DECIMINAL CLASSIFICATION SYSTEM

000–099
GENERALITIES (Encyclopedias, Bibliographies, Periodicals, Journals)

100–199
PHILOSOPHY (Conduct)

200–299
RELIGION

300–399
SOCIAL STUDIES (Economics, Sociology, Civics, Law, Education, Vocations, Customs)

400–499
LANGUAGES (Dictionaries, Grammar)

500–599
SCIENCES (Mathematics, Astronomy, Physics, Chemistry, Geology, Biology, Zoology, Botany)

600–699
TECHNOLOGY (Medicine, Engineering, Agriculture, Business, Television, Aviation)

700–799
THE ARTS (Architecture, Sculpture, Painting, Music, Photography)

800–899
LITERATURE (Novels, Poetry, Plays)

900–999
GEOGRAPHY AND HISTORY

KNOWLEDGE is a rainbow of experiences rich with color, sound, and texture.
READING is the primary pathway to learning and gaining KNOWLEDGE.
Parents, give your child the power of KNOWLEDGE through READING.

Coaching Tip

17. Lesson on **RESPONSIBILITY**

> Every family member is responsible for what they think and do. Parents and their children are joint stakeholders in the honor and trust of the family.
>
> *Coaching Tip*

RESPONSIBILITY Lesson Objectives:
- Children will write a definition of RESPONSIBILITY.
- Parents will give their children positive verbal reinforcement.

Parents should:
1. Read the introductory summary of RESPONSIBILITY and discuss how being responsible is of great benefit to the family and its members. Explain how being a responsible person involves hard work and sacrifice. The strong link between responsibility and good character is inescapable. Parent character coaches must be primarily responsible for training their children. Kids that act responsibly and avoid making excuses for themselves exemplify character, reflecting greatly upon their parents.

2. Parent to Child Dialogue (positive verbal reinforcement):

✓ "I trust you."

✓ "You are very responsible."

✓ "I respect you for what you did."

✓ "Thank you for doing what I said."

✓ "I can count on you!"

✓ "You're a reliable person."

✓ "Thanks for coming through even when it got tough."

3. Responsibility requires hard work and effort to get what you want in life. Opportunities come and go, but it is the person who assumes personal responsibility for their actions that is more likely to make the most of what life offers them. To be responsible means that you will make the most of your talents and work to achieve success. Explain how responsibility is a commitment to being the very best that you can be. Kids need to know that life demands a commitment to excellence, and not doing their best is being irresponsible. A responsible person is also a disciplined person. Discuss the challenges of being disciplined in thought and action. To be responsible is your duty. If you simply do your best then you don't have to make any excuses regardless of the final outcome.

RESPONSIBILITY

Parents have the primary responsibility of raising their children. Teaching your children to be accountable for their actions is extremely important. First, parents must teach their kids to always respect their authority. Parents earn this respect by demonstrating their love and commitment to their children. Respect has to be earned. Failing to establish parental authority will create a growing snowball of disrespect that undermines the stability of the family. Effective parents love their children and instill in them respect for authority, both inside and outside the family. Children who obey family rules have little difficulty in coping with school rules and later with the four adult roles.

In my opinion, the widespread erosion of responsibility throughout society is directly traceable to the declining ability of parents to teach and enforce this essential life skill. Change and disruption is a daily staple with parents struggling to meet a rising tide of challenges and responsibilities. Many families are being swept along, fragmented and unable to create a domestic situation where consistent respect and responsibility can gain a firm foothold. Responsibility demands that parents take a stand to train their children, and send them into the world with the gift of discipline and a commitment to doing their duty. No educational reform can truly overcome unruly and irresponsible children.

❖ **A person's ability to shoulder an array of responsibilities is their true measure. Parents must meet their responsibility in raising their children to be responsible for themselves and believing in duty, honor and family.**

NO EXCUSES!

RESPONSIBILTY—"No Excellence Without Labor"
William Wirt
Lesson 71, *McGuffey's Fifth Eclectic Reader*

NO EXCELLENCE WITHOUT LABOR
1. The education, moral and intellectual, of every individual, must chiefly be his own work. Rely upon it that the ancients were right; both in morals and intellect we give the final shape to our characters, and thus become, emphatically, the architects of our fortune. How else could it happen that young men, who have had precisely the same opportunities, should be continually presenting us with such different results, and rushing to such opposite destinies?

2. Differences in talent will not solve it, because that difference is very often in favor of the disappointed candidate. You will see issuing from the walls of the same college, nay, sometimes from the bosom of the same family, two young men, of whom one will be admitted to be a genius of high order, the other scarcely above the point of mediocrity; yet you will see the genius sinking and perishing in poverty, obscurity, and wretchedness; while on the other hand, you will observe the mediocre plodding his slow but sure way up the hill of life, gaining steadfast footing at every step, and mounting, at length, to eminence and distinction, an ornament to his family, a blessing to his country.

3. Now, whose work is this? Manifestly their own. They are the architects of their respective fortunes. The best seminary of learning that can open its portals to you can do no more than to afford you the opportunity of instruction; but it must depend, at last, on yourselves, whether you will be instructed or not, or to what point you will push your instruction.

4. And of this be assured, I speak from observation a certain truth: THERE IS NO EXCELLENCE WITHOUT GREAT LABOR. It is the fiat of fate, from which no power of genius can absolve you.

5. Genius and laziness is like the poor moth that flutters around a candle till it scorches itself to death. If genius be desirable at all, it is only that great and magnanimous kind, which, like the condor of South America, pitches from the summit of Chimborazo, above the clouds, and sustains itself at pleasure in that empyreal region with an energy rather invigorated than weakened by the effort.

RESPONSIBILITY—Questions:

1. This fifth grade level reading dates from 1879. What surprises you about this essay? Were there any vocabulary challenges?

2. Does being a genius automatically assure a person of success and acclaim?

3. How much responsibility do we have being "architects of own fortune?"

4. What is meant by being "an ornament to his family" in the reading?

5. What is your primary responsibility to your own family? Why should the phrase, "I don't care," be forever banned?

NO EXCUSES ACTIVITY

> A family that instills discipline and duty in its children, I feel, is at the forefront of solving the greatest social crisis of our time. Parents, coach your kids in lessons of responsibility.
>
> *Coaching Tip*

Children should:
- List all of their family responsibilities.
- Explain the difference between telling the truth and making an excuse.
- Design a responsibility conveying the ideas of duty, honor and family.

❖ **ASSIGNMENT: Help your children determine their family responsibilities. Discuss why the "no excuses option" is the way to go and complete a responsibility poster.**

1. **Children will be able to determine their responsibilities to the family.** Kids have an obligation to perform duty to their family, which is an unconditional commitment. Parents and children should each take a blank piece of paper and challenge each other by listing different things they are responsible for in the family. Parents have the primary responsibility of providing for the general welfare of the family, such as food, clothing, shelter and protection. Children are responsible for their own conduct and discipline. Duties extend to self-care and maintenance of the home. Every family member must carryout responsibilities if they expect to benefit and enjoy the privilege of being part of a family.

2. **After discussing why telling the truth and being responsible is important, children will be able to explain why making no excuses is the best life strategy.** Some key discussion points:

- Responsible people tell the truth.

- It is easier to remember the truth.

- An excuse is really a concealment of the truth.

- An excuse is a "crutch" or an easy way out.

- Be truthful and don't make excuses.

3. **Parents should assist their children in making a "Duty, Honor and Family" poster.** Each of these three elements should be defined, with brief sentences completing the following opening statements as part of the poster.

DUTY is important because . . .
HONOR means that I will . . .
FAMILY requires that I . . .

A basic triangle design can be used on the poster listing the three elements. Pictures clipped from magazines can also be used to illustrate the poster. Make it colorful and hang it up.

DUTY, HONOR, FAMILY

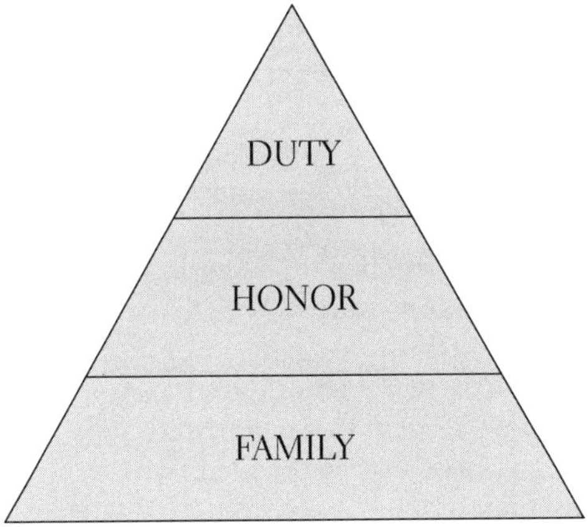

JOURNAL: GREATEST STORIES

A Championship Family needs to connect itself to its own special narrative which is a collection of stories passed down through generations combining to create a unique and fascinating family history.

FAMILY **STORYTELLING**

FAMILY **SHORT STORIES**

FAMILY **HISTORY**

FAMILY STORYTELLING

Journal Assignment: All family members will participate in orally telling a family story. Oral storytelling is a time honored tradition that reaches back into our most distant past. Front porches or backyard gatherings are nice venues for this "ancient ritual." There is nothing quite like "reeling yarns" to share experiences between the generations. Usually, oral stories are modified and embellished over time but that's okay. Oral stories should be recorded and can be transcribed.

Some suggestions for Family Storytelling:

- Are there any "family legends" that can be shared?
- Any "family immigration" stories? We are all immigrants from other places and times.
- Any special grandparent stories or questions you might have?
- Are there any "love stories" that can be recalled?
- What humorous stories can be recalled?
- Are there any memorable family sayings or quotes that have been passed on?
- Has anyone endured any hardships or adverse situations?
- Any family "war stories" that can be told?
- What about "golden memories" of the family?
- Any notable achievements involving the family?

- Everyone can recall prior experiences with family and friends.
- Don't forget family "folk tales" that may or may not have happened.

FAMILY SHORT STORIES

Journal Assignment: All family members write a family short story. The story could be based on something heard during a family storytelling session. Kids often have a fear of writing because of spelling and grammar, but word processing has opened the door to writing as never before. Parents need to assist their children with starting to write at an early age. Get the kids on the keyboard! Stories can be illustrated with photos and drawings.

- **Person is the "voice" used to tell the story.** First person is the use of "I" in the story. For example, "I remember going to the beach." Second person is "You went to the mountains." Third person is "She made a trip to the desert." Most fiction is written in the third person, while most personal recollections are done in the first.

- **Dialogue is conversation between two or more people.** This technique is very effective in making stories more realistic and interesting. Look for samples in novels.

- **Balance is the blending of narrative and dialogue in a story.** This technique takes a lot of practice to perfect.

- **The title of your story should capture interest and convey what the story is about in some manner.** Titles can be a single word or several. Some samples:

"Day of the Tsunami"
"Survival in the Mountains"
"Desert Showdown"
"The Great BBQ Cook-off"
"When Mom & Dad Got Married"
"When Sparky Got Loose!"
"Surprise at Disneyland"
"Mystery at the Mall"
"UFO's Over the Neighborhood"

Story Title ______________________________

Author ______________________

Beginning (Introduction):

Main Body of Story (Details of story):

Conclusion (Surprise ending?):

FAMILY HISTORY

Journal Assignment: All family members will research some family history and write an article of their findings. Researching the family's distant past can be very exciting. A deeper sense of family can be gained by going back to a much different time and place to find out what your relatives did and experienced.

- **Interviewing** parents, grandparents and great grandparents is a good way to unlock the past. Ask lots of questions. Prepare your questions in advance when asking about their childhoods, memories of where they grew up, schooling, family and friends, homes, their community, trips, vacations and local history.

• **Photographs** offer a gold mine of family information. So many old photos go unlabeled, so ask questions to help identify and date them. A box of black and white photos can be an incredible find! Old photos can now be restored and scanned into a computer database.

• **Internet investigations** can provide a wealth of family information. This database of information is increasing daily. Some good starting points are: ancestry.com, geneaology.com, ellisisland.com and family.search.org.

• **Family time lines** should be made from every family member. From a birth date on, this recording of major life events can serve as a story outline to be filled in with family research. Dates, people, places and events all serve as reference points helping to reveal many stories. Always be on the lookout for diaries, journals, old family Bibles, letters, newspaper articles, school programs, notes, announcements and cards.

Family History Article Title ______________________________

____

Researcher ____________________________

Beginning (Introduction):

Main Body of Story (Details of story):

Conclusion (Summary):

Footnotes:

Sources (Bibliography):

CHAPTER FOUR

GAME TIME: (Life Skills)

Now the time has come for the CHAMPIONSHIP FAMILY to literally "walk the talk" as they come onto the playing field of life. To win as a family, everyone must demonstrate the combined life skills of DECISION MAKING, LEADERSHIP, ORGANIZATION, SERVICE, TACT, TEAMWORK and VIRTUE. It all comes together in the daily action of striving and living as a family. **GAME TIME is where parents and children have the opportunity to:**

- Execute LIFE SKILLS.
- Display effective and timely **DECISION MAKING.**
- Show their determined **LEADERSHIP.**
- Exhibit their practices of **ORGANIZATION.**
- Engage in and support others through acts of **SERVICE.**
- Never forget the supreme importance of **TACT.**
- Use the power and impact of **TEAMWORK.**
- Live a life faithful to the principles of **VIRTUE.**

A Championship Family is successful in its daily games by the combined talents and skills of all of its players. Victories come through the courage and resolve of a family working and playing together, knowing they are special and loved. Whatever life throws at such a family, they know that success can be theirs as long as they hold together and show their remarkable character. It is not so much what happens to these families that is important, but how they react, holding true to their positive and ethical values which are really important.

Coaching Tip

18. Lesson on **DECISION MAKING**

> Parenting and character coaching involve making decisions—some are easy others more difficult—but make the best ones you can.
>
> *Coaching Tip*

Lesson Objectives for DECISION MAKING

- Children will write a definition for DECISION MAKING.
- Parents will give their children positive verbal reinforcement.

Parents should:

1. Read the introductory summary on DECISION MAKING and talk about how this information could be summarized into a short definition. Decisions need to involve thinking everything through before a final one is made. Think things through before acting. In making decisions, consider what is fair to all concerned. In your mind should always be what is good for the entire family. Explain how making choices is a continuous and never ending process that rests heavily upon the values of CHARACTER, MORAL COURAGE, TRUTH, JUDGMENT and RESPONSIBILITY. The values in this book are always interacting with each other.

2. Parent to Child Dialogue (positive verbal reinforcement):

✓ "Good choice!"

✓ "You did an excellent job figuring that out."

✓ "That is the right thing to do."

✓ "Have you considered the consequences?"

✓ "That's fair."

✓ "Awesome choice!"

✓ "You really did your homework on that decision."

3. Discuss how making decisions can be tough with peer pressure. Ignoring what your friends think and feel can be very difficult. Talk about how we all want acceptance from others and to be well thought of. However, explain that when friends make bad choices, they must stand firm in their conviction to do what is right. Going along with the crowd can sometimes mean selling out your values. Good decision making requires thinking for yourself and doing what your values compel you to do. Decisions should follow a logical analysis and process, and must mirror your own true courage and belief system.

DECISION MAKING

As a parent, your role in striving to make good choices and decisions for your family is a twenty-four hour, seven day a week job. No time outs or vacations from deciding things. Making "24/7" decisions is unrelenting, and when you throw in "staying true to your values" while being consistent, you have the makings for the ultimate challenge. Does this call for superhuman powers? No, it calls for the best of character parenting. As your child's character coach, you must walk the talk as you demonstrate daily just how the decision making process is done. Let your kids see you performing at your best.

Good decision making depends on a process that can handle the short and long term, the unexpected and the anticipated. Character coaches are cool under pressure and able to make the hard calls while remaining fair. Sometimes things have to be negotiated, but never at the cost of your core values. Your primary concern is the safety and welfare of your family. A good rule of thumb is to follow the rules and to exercise common sense which strangely is not so common! Mentor your kids as they make their own decisions. Coach and train them actively in this skill.

❖ **One of life's constant challenges is making good and timely decisions. Remember, that not making a decision is actually making one.**

THINK THEN ACT!

> Championship Families are the direct result of good decisions. All family members need to make positive and enthusiastic decisions.
>
> *Coaching Tip*

DECISION MAKING—"True Courage"
Lesson 52, *McGuffey's Third Eclectic Reader*

TRUE COURAGE
One cold winter's day, three boys were passing by a schoolhouse. The oldest was a bad boy, always in trouble himself, and trying to get others into trouble. The youngest was George. He was a very good boy.

George wished to do right, but was very much wanting in courage. The other boys were named Henry and James. As they walked along, they talked as follows:

Henry. What fun it would be to throw a snowball against the schoolroom door, and make the teacher and scholars all jump!

James. You would jump, if you should. If the teacher did not catch you and whip you, he would tell your father, and you would get whipped then; and that would make you jump higher than the scholars, I think.

Henry. Why, we would get so far off, before the teacher could come to the door, that he could not tell who we are. Here is a snowball just as hard as ice, and George would as soon throw it against the door as not.

James. Give it to him, and see. He would not dare to throw it.

Henry. Do you think George is a coward? You do not know him as well as I do. Here, George, take this snowball, and show James that you are not such a coward as he thinks you are.

George. I am not afraid to throw it; but I do not want to. I do not see that it will do any good, or that there will be any fun in it.

James. There! I told you he would not dare to throw it.

Henry. Why, George, are you turning coward? I thought you did not fear anything. Come, save your credit, and throw it. I know you are not afraid.

George. Well, I am not afraid to throw. Give me the snowball. I would as soon throw it as not.

Whack! went the snowball against the door; and the boys took to their heels. Henry was laughing as heartily as he could, to think what a fool he had made of George.

George had a whipping for his folly, as he ought to have had. He was such a coward, that he was afraid of being called a coward. He did not dare refuse to do as Henry told him, for fear that he would be laughed at.

If he had been really a brave boy, he would have said, "Henry, do you suppose that I am foolish as to throw that snowball, just because you want to have me. You may throw your own snowballs, if you please!"

Henry would, perhaps, have laughed at him, and called him a coward.

But George would have said, "Do you think that I care for your laughing? I do not think it's right to throw the snowball. I will not do that which I think to be wrong, if the whole town should join with you in laughing."

This would have been real courage. Henry would have seen, at once, that it would do no good to laugh at a boy who has so bold a heart. You must have this fearless spirit, or you will get into trouble, and will be, and ought to be, disliked by all.

Questions:

1. What fun idea did Henry come up with?

2. How did Henry and James talk George into throwing the snowball?

3. Why did George do it and what were the consequences?

4. How could George have handled the situation differently?

5. Do you have the courage to resist peer pressure and do what you feel is *the* right thing to do?

SEVEN STEPS Activity

> Making good decisions is determined by your character values, your choices mirror who you are.
>
> *Coaching Tip*

Children should:

- Explain how they solve problems.
- Consider the problem of "procrastination" or putting things off.
- Apply the Seven Steps model to deciding how to eliminate procrastinating.

❖ **ASSIGNMENT: Children explain how they decide, consider how procrastination is a negative practice, and use the Seven Steps model to eliminate this habit.**

1. **Children explain how they would react to a series of statements involved with making decisions and problem solving.** Parents should ask their kids:

- What is the first thing you always do when faced with a problem?
- How do you handle the pressure of a serious problem?
- Are you always able to think calmly and define the real problem?
- Do you go for the quick and easy solution?
- Do you put off making a decision for as long as possible?
- When solving a problem, do you listen to your conscience?
- Do you carefully consider all possible solutions?
- Do you let your friends influence how you decide things?
- Are you usually happy with your decisions? Why or why not?

2. **Parents help their kids consider the problem of "procrastination."** To procrastinate is to put things off to the very last minute. This generally causes poor work and delaying a tough job only makes it tougher. Delaying could be the greatest single barrier to effective deci-

sion making. Good decisions depend on you being a self-starter and making timely decisions. Getting started allows you to go through the Seven Steps to better reach the best possible decision.

Why do people procrastinate?

- They feel tired and lazy.
- They hope that if they ignore the problem, it will go away.
- They don't know how to begin or what to do.
- They are comfortable with waiting things out.
- They don't like what they may have to do.
- They feel overwhelmed by the problem.
- They are afraid because they fear making a mistake and failing.
- They have made procrastination a habit – it's easier to wait.

3. **Parents will assist in eliminating the problem of "procrastination;" thereby demonstrating how the SEVEN STEPS MODEL can work.** Read through the following case study on procrastination and then proceed through the decision making steps. Any problem can be handled in the same manner. To get rid of procrastination is to open the way for more effective decision making now and in the future.

CASE STUDY: "THE MATH FLASH CARDS"

Sally is a fourth grader who has had problems with her math assignments. She doesn't like to do math and is falling behind. Her teacher, Mrs. Jones, has given Sally a special homework assignment to help her learn multiplication tables from 1 × 1 up to 12 × 12. Mrs. Jones gave Sally a set of multiplication flash cards to practice over the weekend and a note to her parents asking them to help her practice with the cards. Upon arriving home on Friday, Sally puts the cards and note away and does not tell her parents. Sally wants to put off her homework until Saturday or maybe Sunday. She will give her parents the note later. That night, a friend calls Sally and offers to help her with the homework on Sunday afternoon. Sally agrees to this.

Parents, discuss these questions with your child:

- What is the problem?
- Is Sally procrastinating? Why?
- Is Sally making a good decision?
- Do you think Sally feels good about her decision?
- What will be the consequences if Sally waits as late as Sunday night to tell her parents about the homework assignment?
- What if Sally ignores the assignment completely and does nothing?

Parents should go through the SEVEN STEPS Model with their children, answering the questions and determining which of the following decisions are best:

A— Sally should practice using the flash cards by herself.

B— Sally should wait until Saturday night to tell her parents.

C— Sally should have her friend help her practice.

D— Sally should immediately give the note and cards to her parents.

E— Sally should tell her parents on Saturday and let them know she is going to have a friend help her.

> Train your child to avoid procrastination. Immediate action is the first step in decision making.
>
> *Coaching Tip*

SEVEN STEPS MODEL

This is a basic DECISION MAKING template which can be used to deal with any problem. The first critical operation is to state exactly what the problem is. If this cannot be done, the following steps will not adequately address the situation or necessarily lead to a good choice.

PROBLEM STATEMENT:

____

____

____

STEP ONE: THINKING CLEARLY & FOCUSING

(Look directly and objectively at the problem.)

- WHAT IS THE PROBLEM?
- CAN YOU WRITE THE PROBLEM IN ONE OR TWO SENTENCES?
- IS THIS REALLY THE PROBLEM?
- IS ANYTHING BEING OVERLOOKED?

STEP TWO: IDENTIFY THE UNDERLYING CAUSES OF THE PROBLEM

(Analyzing problems are challenging but accuracy here is critical.)

- WHAT ARE THE DIFFERENT PARTS OF THE PROBLEM?
- WHAT CAUSED IT?
- WILL IT GO AWAY BY ITSELF?
- WILL THIS PROBLEM KEEP HAPPENING?

STEP THREE: IDENTIFY NEEDED RESOURCES

(Do a complete inventory of assets.)

- CAN YOU GET ADVICE?
- COULD YOU COLLABORATE WITH SOMEONE?
- IS THERE SOMETHING YOU NEED TO SOLVE THE PROBLEM?
- CAN YOU GET WHAT YOU NEED?

STEP FOUR: CONSIDER ALL POSSIBLE SOLUTIONS AND RANK THEM

(Think creatively and methodically.)

- LIST ALL POSSIBLE SOLUTIONS
- COMPARE THEIR ADVANTAGES AND DISADVANTAGES
- CONSIDER CHOICES FROM ALL ANGLES
- RANK SOLUTIONS FROM BEST TO WORST

STEP FIVE: CHARACTER VALUE CHECKS

(See FIVE TESTS Activity in Lesson 15 on JUDGMENT.)

- GOLDEN RULE
- ETHICS TEST
- INTEGRITY TEST
- ETHICS ALWAYS
- PRESS RELEASE

STEP SIX: SELECT BEST CHOICE AND IMPLEMENT!

(Give choice your full support.)

- REVIEW YOUR SOLUTION
- SUPPORT YOUR CHOICE!
- IMPLEMENT WITH ENTHUSIASM!
- FOLLOW THROUGH AS NEEDED

STEP SEVEN: EVALUATE YOUR SOLUTION—DID IT WORK?

(Evaluate your results and continue the SEVEN STEP Model if the problem persists or new ones have broken out.)

- EXAMINE RESULTS
- GET FULL PERSPECTIVE
- IS EVERYTHING OKAY?
- IF PROBLEM CONTINUES—GO BACK TO STEP ONE AND REPEAT

19. Lesson on **LEADERSHIP**

> Parents as your family leaders, always look back to make sure that the kids are really following you!
>
> ***Coaching Tip***

LEADERSHIP Lesson Objectives:
- Children will write a definition of LEADERSHIP.
- Parents will give their children positive verbal reinforcement.

Parents should:
1. Read the introductory summary on LEADERSHIP and help their kids write a short definition for this term. While parents are the primary leaders of their family, it is vital for them to display their leadership skills and teach those skills to their children. Leaders are not born, but they develop these skills over time. Leadership is a learned skill, which is why parents need to properly model it and coach their children in learning to be leaders themselves.

2. Parent to Child Dialogue (positive verbal reinforcement):

✓ "Follow me!"

✓ "Listen to my instructions."

✓ "I'll show you the way."

✓ "You've got what it takes."

✓ "You're growing up, I see you as a leader."

✓ "This family is full of leaders."

✓ "Okay, lead on!"

3. After reading William Tyler Page's "The American Creed," discuss how this was written in 1917 with the entry of the United States into World War I. This was a time of intense American patriotism as U.S. troops started to go overseas to France to fight against Germany. You may need to do some research into World War I so you can explain its causes, general conduct, and outcome with your kids. Leaders must believe in a positive system of principles and values to display moral leadership. Refer back to Lesson 5 on RESPECT and the "Pledge of Allegiance." Compare the Creed with the Pledge. The Creed is a statement of duty to America while the Pledge is a verbal statement of obligation and loyalty to the United States.

> Kids must learn to follow before they can successfully lead.
>
> ***Coaching Tip***

LEADERSHIP

Parents are the leaders of their families and this role of leadership must be vigorously assumed and pursued. Parental leadership is at the heart of the Championship Family. Good leadership gives a family self-assurance and self-reliance while poor leadership undermines all that a family can be. Just as a parent must be prepared to sacrifice for their children, an effective parent leader must continually sacrifice for the family. Parent leaders serve those he or she is leading. The relationship between LEADERSHIP and SERVICE is extremely close, as successful leaders are very good at serving and meeting the needs of their followers.

Parents as leaders are guardians of their children. They should not rise above the ceiling of their own character. The key is to never lose sight of your values and always be there to advise your children. If leadership is influencing others, than be a good and steady influence in the lives of your children. John C. Maxwell, author of *The 21 Irrefutable Laws of Leadership*, rates integrity as the most important ingredient of leadership. Integrity takes time to attain but can be lost in an instant of bad judgment. Maxwell says, "When I have integrity, my words and deeds match up. I am who I am, no matter where I am or who I am with." Character Parenting is leadership of the heart and mind, guided by character values with integrity as the leading edge. Parents as leadership coaches must be assertive and daring, willing to hold themselves and family members accountable for their behavior.

❖ **Skills of leadership can be learned and practiced, empowering a family to display extraordinary courage and character. Active parents who act as leaders demonstrate and teach their children leadership skills.**

SHOW THE WAY!

> Family members keep a close eye on each other. Parents, as you lead your family, just know that you are on stage every minute!
>
> *Coaching Tip*

LEADERSHIP—THE AMERICAN CREED
William Tyler Page

I believe in the United States of America
as government of the people by the people,
for the people, whose just powers are
derived from a republic, a sovereign Nation
of many sovereign States; a perfect Union
one and inseparable; established upon those
principles of freedom, equality, justice and
humanity for which American patriots
sacrificed their lives and fortunes. I therefore
believe it is my duty to my country to love
it, to support its Constitution, to obey its
laws, to respect its flag and to defend it
against all enemies.
—William Tyler Page

Questions:
1. What does the American Creed say to you?

2. The American Creed calls for unconditional duty to the country. Do you believe unconditional duty also applies to the family?

3. What duty does the President of the United States have?

4. What duty does a parent have?

5. Given the example of the American Creed, can your family write its own "Family Creed" or statement of duty?

GREATEST PRESIDENTS ACTIVITY

Children should:
- Consider the elements of American Presidential greatness and see how these same leadership qualities apply to parents.
- Research an American President examining their leadership strengths and weaknesses.
- Select an American President and explain why you think they should be considered to be great.

❖ **ASSIGNMENT: Parents help their kids consider qualities of Presidential leadership greatness, and then select an American President they feel to be a great leader.**

1. **Parents work with their children in evaluating elements of Presidential greatness.** What qualities contribute to calling anyone great? While the office of the American Presidency is esteemed, not all Presidents have been considered to be great. Many have fallen far short of this. Discuss:

☐ CHARACTER: Values shown through words and deeds.

☐ PERSEVERANCE: Evidence of trying to achieve and never giving up.

☐ MORAL COURAGE: Examples of standing up for values despite the odds.

☐ JUDGMENT: Examples of making good choices consistent with values.

☐ LEADERSHIP: Evidence of taking charge and giving good direction.

☐ VIRTUE: Moral excellence exhibited in words and deeds.

The values listed above constitute a vigorous test for anyone. A leader is in a relentless pursuit of excellence in performance. Leadership is a journey—not a final destination. Parents of a Championship Family are in a never ending pursuit of leadership excellence.

2. **Consider a recent ranking of American Presidents and discuss its findings.** This offers a starting point in considering how Presidents can be rated and ranked. No ranking of American Presidents can be considered perfect or final. History continues to re-evaluate Presidents with the passing of time. Presidents that rank extremely low have little chance to rise significantly now or in the future. It is doubtful that James Buchanan or Warren Harding can ever be expected to surpass George Washington or Abraham Lincoln in any Presidential greatness poll. In your rankings discussion consider:

- Who are the top three? Why do you think they are on top?
- Who is at the bottom listed as failures? Why are they ranked so low?

- How have Twentieth Century Presidents done? Who are the top five?
- How many presidents have been assassinated?
- Who served longest as President?
- Who served the shortest terms?

3. **Select a President that you feel should be the "Greatest American President."** In making your choice consider the elements of greatness criteria already discussed: CHARACTER, PERSEVERANCE, MORAL COURAGE, JUDGMENT, LEADERSHIP and VIRTUE. It's okay if family members choose the same President to honor. You may wonder who will be considered the greatest President of the 21st Century. It could be someone not even born yet.

GREATEST AMERICAN PRESIDENT

MY GREATEST PRESIDENT IS: ______________________________

THIS PRESIDENT IS THE GREATEST BECAUSE OF:

CHARACTER

PERSEVERANCE

MORAL COURAGE

JUDGMENT

LEADERSHIP

VIRTUE

IF I WERE PRESIDENT, THESE ARE JUST SOME OF THE THINGS I WOULD DO IN MY HUNDRED DAYS IN OFFICE:

20. Lesson on **ORGANIZATION**

> A Championship Family must become organized and clutter free to be set free.
>
> ***Coaching Tip***

ORGANIZATION Lesson Objectives:

- Children will write a definition of ORGANIZATION.
- Parents will give their children positive verbal reinforcement.

Parents should:

1. Read the introductory summary on ORGANIZATION, and assist children in writing a brief definition of this essential skill. Being an organized person is a lifelong challenge as everyone is faced with time and material management issues. Using the most of each day is no small task. Time and logistics challenges require an organized plan which can hopefully prioritize and focus our efforts. We all have too many material possessions and breaking the grip of "accumulated chaos" requires a united family effort.

2. Parent to Child Dialogue (positive verbal reinforcement)

✓ "Thanks for cleaning up your room."

✓ "Let's put it on your calendar."

✓ "You're getting organized!"

✓ "Thank you for helping me with the sorting."

✓ "You're a good organizer."

✓ "You've done an awesome job using your time wisely."

✓ "Wow, unbelievable job organizing."

3. Talk with your kids about how they keep their time and materials organized. What habits and practices does the family have in regards to organization? Can you readily find things? Could the family be better organized? How? If you don't know where things are, they are of little use to you. Kids need to see that valuable time is wasted if you're constantly looking for things that you know you have but cannot find. That is why the "everything in its place" strategy is a good one. When you buy something, either it is used up or stored. The consumables take care of themselves but the storing or display of material "stuff" is a continuing challenge. Many people play the "paper chase" game, an endless quest to find that one piece of paper. A good organization system is one that keeps "law and order" at home, school and work.

> Train your kids to toss and to let go of what is unneeded. You can't keep everything—so keep the indispensable and unload the rest!
>
> *Coaching Tip*

ORGANIZATION

An organized home has a calming and soothing effect on the entire family. A clutter-free environment has a positive influence on your ability to concentrate and to think. An organized family has been freed to really live with renewed energy and stamina. Efficiency through organization improves the quality and productivity of our lives. Organization is a skill that character coaches both practice and teach their children. It's not enough to tell the kids to clean up their rooms when the rest of the house is sinking under a blizzard of clutter. For it to work, clutter control must be practiced from the front to back door and everyplace in between.

Organizing how you work requires a good time management plan and effective work habits. To organize material possessions is simply following a good working plan for the display, control, storage and disposal of all materials that you come in contact with. This requires a degree of discipline and order. Habits of organization help families feel better about themselves and enhance what they can do. Chaos drains away our energy while order increases our capacity to get things done. Organization is the benchmark of a family that has been freed to work and play with greater enthusiasm!

❖ **Organization cuts through accumulative chaos and allows ready access to a richer life. Organized people think clearer and perform at higher levels because they have been freed to do so.**

ORGANIZE FOR SUCCESS

> Before you go after your kids to clean up their closets, take a good look at your own!
>
> *Coaching Tip*

ORGANIZATION—"A Place for Everything"
Lesson 58, *McGuffey's Second Eclectic Reader*

A PLACE FOR EVERYTHING
Mary. I wish you would lend me your thimble, Sarah.
I can never find my own.
Sarah. Why is it, Mary, you can never find it?
Mary. How can I tell? But if you will not lend me yours,
I can borrow one elsewhere.
Sarah. I am willing to lend mine to you, Mary.
But I would very much like to know why you come
to me to borrow so often.
Mary. Because you never lose any of your things, and
always know where to find them.
Sarah. And why do I always know where to find my things?
Mary. I do not know why, I am sure. If I did know,
I might sometimes find my own.
Sarah. I will tell you a secret. I have a place for everything,
and I put everything in its place when I am done using it.

Mary. Well, Sarah, I will never borrow from you again, you may depend upon it.

Sarah. You are not offended with me, I hope.

Mary. No, but I am ashamed. Before night, I will have a place for everything, and then I will keep everything in its place. You have taught me a lesson I shall remember.

ORGANIZATION—Questions:

1. What was Mary's problem?

2. What was Sarah's secret?

3. How well organized are you at home and at school?

4. Does organization require time and effort?

5. What are the rewards for being well organized?

CLUTTER FREE ACTIVITY

> Recycling of paper, cardboard, glass/plastic bottles and aluminum cans must be a joint-family enterprise with everyone taking part in this activity.
>
> *Coaching Tip*

Children should:

- Help conduct a total house and garage clutter survey.
- Develop and implement a monthly family calendar with the rest of the family and a personal space organization plan.
- Assist with planning and doing a family garage sale.

❖ **ASSIGNMENT: Children assist their parents with a clutter survey, help with a family calendar, organize their own space and possessions and participate in a family garage sale.**

1. **Family members conduct a clutter survey going through the house and garage.** Parents will maintain a master clipboard as each room is investigated for clutter or unwanted materials. Items that have been identified as clutter will need to be given a classification: 1) GARAGE SALE ITEM; 2) DONATION ITEM; 3) RECYCLING ITEM; 4) TRASH ITEM.

Clutter Survey Questions:

- **What should go and how?** Example: Piles of magazines in living room should be listed as a RECYCLING ITEM.
- **What should stay but where?** Example: Board games and puzzles in family room could be stored and put away, sold at a GARAGE SALE or given away as a DONATION ITEM.
- **How can clutter be kept from accumulating?** Example: Incoming mail keeps piling up. The solution could involve setting up a routine where mail is routinely sorted, with discards becoming a RECYCLING ITEM. To guard against identity theft, personal and address information should be shredded then recycled.
- **How could a room function better?** Example: Kitchen countertops are cluttered. Solution would be to clear the countertops and keep them ready for food preparation.

2. **Kids help with the Family Monthly Calendar and plan their own personal space organization plan.** Both family time and possessions need to be organized for maximum efficiency.

FAMILY MONTHLY CALENDAR

- Parents will purchase a large wall calendar that has daily boxes large enough to enter events.
- Family members will be instructed to enter their activities on this master family planning calendar.
- All family activities will be marked with a yellow highlighter to remind family members when they have been scheduled. These are priority events.
- Parents will resolve schedule conflicts and all family members will be expected to refer to the calendar and keep up to date on activities.

PERSONAL SPACE ORGANIZATION PLAN

- Children will consider rearranging their bedroom area furniture. Any changes will be coordinated with their parents. Changes can help with organizing.
- Clothing management requires either hanging, placement in drawers, or consignment to the laundry. No clothing piles are permitted to exist.
- Toys, books and other items will be shelved or stored. All need designated places. Some of these items can be identified for the garage sale or donated.
- Children will write their room cleaning schedule and post it on the wall. This will include dusting, sweeping, vacuuming and trash removal.

3. **The family plans, organizes and conducts their own garage sale for "fun and profit."** This culminating activity is where the family officially lets go of unwanted clutter, recovers more control over their home, and turns a little profit in the process. I think the average American home has excessive clutter that needs to be pared down. After conducting the clutter survey, it probably has become apparent that many items should be part of a garage sale.

ANTIQUE and COLLECTIBLE WARNING!

Although the goal is to get rid of unwanted things, be careful when selling anything that falls into the category of a valuable antique or collectible. That old, dusty vase or forgotten box of baseball cards just might have greater value than you realize. Real treasures can be hiding amid the clutter you are trying to get rid of. True heirlooms should be handed down, but be selective about what qualifies for this special status.

> Kids can learn many business skills through participation in a family garage sale.
>
> *Coaching Tip*

Family Garage Sale Checklist:

_____ Identify and list all GARAGE SALE ITEMS from Family Clutter Survey already completed. Place items in boxes and locate in a central staging area.

_____ If the quantity appears to be small, the garage sale could be postponed or a combined sale with another family or two might be considered.

_____ Every sale item must have a price on it. Going to other garage sales can be helpful with pricing and display ideas. Be prepared to handle people who may want to barter.

_____ Advertise by placing garage sale signs around the neighborhood, but remember to take them all down when the sale is done. Weekends are good times to hold garage sales as more people are out and about looking for great bargains.

_____ Plan the basic garage sale setup in advance. Driveways are commonly used for garage sales. All sale items need to be cleaned and made as presentable as possible.

_____ Tables can be used for randomly priced items. It helps to get the "merchandise" off the ground. In fact, try and avoid stacking or laying a lot of things on the ground.

_____ A family garage sale should be an "adventure" for everyone and having fun is important. A positive attitude and enthusiasm are key to a successful experience.

_____ **Maintain strict parental control of the garage sale cash box.** Never leave it unattended and start the sale with lots of smaller bills to help make change. When the sale is over, tally your cash drawer to determine exactly how much money was made. A follow-up family meeting will need help to decide what the garage sale money should be used for. This money could be used for a family outing, party, or to help purchase something the family has wanted for a long time.

GARAGE SALE TODAY

GIGANTIC GARAGE SALE

Garage Sale
at 123 Main St.

GARAGE SALE
of the CENTURY

GARAGE SALE!
Everything Must Go!

21. Lesson on **SERVICE**

> Parents, train your children in the value of service. Serving others is the greatest life skill.
>
> *Coaching Tip*

SERVICE Lesson Objectives:

- Children will write a definition of SERVICE.
- Parents will give their children positive verbal reinforcement.

Parents should:

1. Read the introductory summary on SERVICE and assist their kids in writing a good definition for this pivotal value. Pivotal is how this value changes both the lives of those who serve and those who are served. Kids learn that serving needs to become an automatic response whenever an opportunity for service exists. Their response must be quick and decisive. The secret of serving is that while you should never expect anything in return, you will be rewarded through appreciation and satisfaction. Parents who actively serve in the home and community send a strong message to their kids. Service to others sets in motion a powerful chain reaction that can change lives, and thereby change the world.

2. Parent to Child Dialogue (positive verbal reinforcement):

✓ "Wait, let me help you."

✓ "Thanks for helping others without being told to."

✓ "You've made a great difference!"

✓ "What a help you are to others. Good job!"

✓ "You're really a good friend."

✓ "Thanks for your help, it means a lot to me."

✓ "I respect you for helping other people."

3. Parents need to mentor and monitor their young children as they learn the skills of serving both in and out of the home. Kids need to know that many people have had difficult lives or have special needs. A serving act, a kind word or good deed can make an incredible difference in the life of a disadvantaged or needy person. We never really know just how far an act of service to someone else will go in changing their life. Discuss how different the world would be if people gave to others instead of trying to take. Life's greatest gift is to have the opportunity to give and assist other people. A Championship Family thrives as a team of servers, seeking ways to better their community.

> Parents, instruct your children in the life practice of valuing giving over receiving.
>
> *Coaching Tip*

SERVICE

Acts of service to the family, by its members, are one of the greatest outcomes of Character Parenting. For parents and children to be in mutual support of one another is an empowering enterprise that will lead to incredible outcomes. Family service is a bonding and unifying force that moves the family from the ordinary to the extraordinary! Parents set the tempo by performing service in and outside the family. They are modeling a powerful habit that will forever influence the behavior of their children. Service is one of life's most powerful secrets, and when it is unleashed, lives are never the same. The basic lesson is that all of us cannot truly grow beyond ourselves until we have practiced the habit of serving others.

Character Parenting is centered on servant leadership. The best parents serve their children by meeting their support as well as character education needs. The payback for serving others is immense. An extension of mutual service in the family is volunteering in the community. Making a difference is truly achieved by assisting and helping others whenever and wherever you can. A first priority is for parents to serve their families. A second priority is for kids to learn the many skills of serving. A third priority is to engage in service to the community. Service is a learned skill that with practice becomes a lifelong habit and a shining benchmark of success.

❖ **The greatest secret of personal fulfillment and satisfaction in life is to serve others in the family and in the community. The more you give to others, the more you will get back!**

GIVE TO RECEIVE

> True champions know how to serve others. Service to others is always repaid in so many unimaginable ways.
>
> *Coaching Tip*

SERVICE—"Lend a Hand"
Lesson 6, *McGuffey's Third Eclectic Reader*

LEND A HAND
1.
Lend a hand to one another
In the daily toil of life;
When we meet a weaker brother,
Let us help him in the strife.
There is none so rich but may,
In his turn, be forced to borrow;
And the poor man's lot to-day
May become our own to-morrow.

2.
Lend a hand to one another;
In the race for Honor's crown;
Should it fall upon your brother,
Let not envy tear it down.

Lend a hand to all, we pray,
In their sunshine or their sorrow;
And the prize they've won to-day
May become our own to-morrow.

SERVICE—Questions:

1. How can we "lend a hand" to someone?

2. Are you always ready and willing to lend a hand to your family and friends?

3. How do you perform service to members of your family?

4. How can you perform service to your community?

5. Is "performing service to others" one of your family rules?

SERVICE ABOVE SELF ACTIVITY

> A Championship Family is ready to serve at home and in the community.
>
> *Coaching Tip*

Children should:

- Compile a list of possible community service projects with their parents' help.
- Select and participate with other family members in a volunteer project.
- Write a story on their volunteer experience.

❖ **ASSIGNMENT: Family members will agree on a community service project and then perform this volunteering activity together. Stories on this experience will then be written.**

Parents should assist their children in putting together a master list of possible community service activities. Go to the www.volunteer-match.com to learn more about how you can volunteer for very worthy causes.

Volunteering Categories:

☐ SCHOOLS
☐ CHURCHES/TEMPLES/SYNAGOGUES
☐ LITERACY PROGRAMS
☐ LIBRARIES
☐ SERVICE CLUBS
☐ LOCAL CHAMBER OF COMMERCE
☐ CHARITIES
☐ FOOD BANK
☐ CONVALESCENT HOMES
☐ ENVIRONMENTAL GROUPS
☐ NEIGHBORHOOD GROUPS
☐ BOTANICAL GARDENS
☐ HUMANE SOCIETY
☐ CITY PARKS AND RECREATION
☐ SENIOR CENTERS

2. **Your selection should represent a good fit for the entire family.** The whole family should be able to participate together as one group. Thoroughly discuss the proposed activity with the entire family. Kids

should not do any volunteering by themselves. Parents need to supervise their children in activities outside of the home. The family volunteering activity could be a one time event or an ongoing series of activities. The volunteering project should be balanced with other family activities.

3. **When the community activity has been concluded, all family members will write a short story about their experiences.** This personal recollection can be placed in the FAMILY JOURNAL. In writing this volunteer story, consider:

- WHAT DID YOU DO? When? Where? How? Why?
- HOW DID THIS BENEFIT PEOPLE?
- HOW DID YOU FEEL ABOUT IT?
- DID YOU FACE ANY CHALLENGES?
- ANY SURPRISES?
- DID THIS EXPERIENCE CHANGE YOU? How? Why?
- DO YOU PLAN TO DO MORE VOLUNTEERING?
- WOULD YOU RECOMMEND THIS ACTIVITY TO OTHERS?

Every act of family community service changes you and your children. Character values mean more when they are put into action!

Coaching Tip

MY VOLUNTEERING STORY

DESCRIBE YOUR COMMUNITY SERVICE ACTIVITY.

THOUGHTS AND FEELINGS ABOUT WHAT YOU DID.

NOTE: Photos can also be included to add to your story. A family group picture taken at the volunteering event must be taken. This helps to chronicle the event.

22. Lesson on **TACT**

> Tactful relationships are essential to peace and harmony in the family.
>
> *Coaching Tip*

TACT Lesson Objectives:

- Children will write a definition of TACT.
- Parents will give their children positive verbal reinforcement.

Parents should:

1. Read the introductory summary on TACT and assist their children in writing a definition for this critical life skill. Being tactful will greatly help with securing peace and harmony in the home, at school, in the workplace, or wherever family members may find themselves as they negotiate the sudden twists and turns of life. Tact uses the other Core and Life Skill Values to impact difficult situations in a positive manner. Emphasize to your kids that being tactful never allows them to employ "any means" to achieve a desired result. Discuss how "tactful diplomacy" would make for a better world.

2. Parent to Child Dialogue (positive verbal reinforcement):

✓ "I understand how you must feel."

✓ "I am listening to you."

✓ "Do you think that is fair?"

✓ "You considered their feelings. You're good."

✓ "Let's discuss this openly and fairly."

✓ "Thanks for sharing that with me."

✓ "Super job on handling a difficult person."

3. Emotions and anger cannot be allowed to control your behavior. Instead, use diplomacy patiently and thoughtfully. Everyone must learn to choose their battles wisely and let tact be your steady shield in times of stress and strain. TACT is not a stand-alone value; it is best used as a grand coalition with other values including CHARACTER, PERSEVERANCE, RESPECT, CARING, FAITH, LOVE, MORAL COURAGE, TRUTH, COMMUNICATION, CONFIDENCE, JUDGMENT, RESPONSIBILITY, DECISION MAKING, TEAMWORK and VIRTUE. This is how a Championship Family thrives and prospers.

> Train kids in how to network character values together to maximize their effectiveness.
>
> *Coaching Tip*

TACT

Displaying sensitivity to the rights of others is an important interpersonal relations skill. Consideration of the feelings and well being of others is a best practice. Tact requires that we guide our thoughts and actions with compassion—never with brute force or unyielding pressure. The ends never justify the means. TACT must be clearly and effectively demonstrated by parents so that their kids can see, hear, and touch it! Tact is the guardian of harmony and respect in the home. The world can sometimes be a very unfair and hostile place, which is why a tactful family is a sanctuary for parents and children alike.

Once children learn how thoughts and actions can be filtered through tact, they can interact with people outside the family in a more positive manner. Behind tact lies a determination to stand up for what is right. The art of diplomacy comes alive with the skillful employment of tact. Arguments are a breakdown of diplomacy. Avoiding arguments takes a true dedication to tact and its allies, but the effort is worth all the work. Tact is a skill that is in short supply in today's world; people seem to only see and care about their own opinions and beliefs. Tact demands complete understanding and cooperation.

❖ **Abusing others with words and deeds reduces and diminishes yourself as a person. Diplomacy is the art of upholding values and the integrity of people.**

SHOW YOUR UNDERSTANDING

> As a parent, don't tear down your children with negative words. Rather, build them up with positive words.
>
> *Coaching Tip*

TACT—"Speak Gently"
George Washington Langford
Lesson 43, *McGuffey's Third Eclectic Reader*

SPEAK GENTLY
1. Speak gently; it is better far
To rule by love than fear:
Speak gently; let no harsh words mar
The good we might do here.

2. Speak gently to the little child;
Its love be sure to gain;
Teach it in accents soft and mild;
It may long remain.

3. Speak gently to the aged one;
Grieve not the careworn heart:
The sands of life are nearly run;
Let such in peace depart.

4. Speak gently, kindly to the poor;
Let no harsh tones be heard;
They have enough they must endure,
Without an unkind word.

TACT—Questions:

1. Who should we "speak gently" to and why?

2. Why should "harsh words" be avoided?

3. What might happen if people spoke more gently in the home, community, nation, and the world?

4. Could you be more tactful with family, friends, and strangers?

5. Is being tactful one of your family rules?

DIPLOMACY GAME ACTIVITY

> Conflict and argument represent a failure of diplomacy. Parents, train your children to be tactful diplomats.
>
> *Coaching Tip*

Children should:

- Define the core values and life skills of diplomatic negotiations.
- Consider the primary sources of family conflict.
- Participate with other family members in the DIPLOMACY GAME.

❖ **ASSIGNMENT: Children will review the core values essential to tact, explore the causes of family conflict, and play the Diplomacy Game.**

1. Referring back to previous lessons, children should provide short definitions for the **CORE VALUES**:

   ABILITY—See Lesson 1
   CHARACTER—See Lesson 2
   RESPECT—See Lesson 5
   CARING—See Lesson 6
   FAITH—See Lesson 8
   LOVE—See Lesson 10
   MORAL COURAGE—See Lesson 11
   TRUTH—See Lesson 12
   RESPONSIBILITY—See Lesson 17
   SERVICE—See Lesson 21
   TACT—See this Lesson
   VIRTUE—See Lesson 24

   LIFE SKILLS VALUES:

   PERSEVERANCE—See Lesson 4
   COMMUNICATION—See Lesson 13
   CONFIDENCE—See Lesson 14
   JUDGMENT—See Lesson 15
   LEADERSHIP—See Lesson 19

It is clear that the CORE VALUES and selected LIFE SKILL VALUES play important roles in combining with TACT in the "art of diplomacy." CHARACTER and TACT are fundamental to any diplomatic conversation. Remember that the values in this book should be used in combinations, not by themselves.

2. Parents should review with their kids some routine causes for family conflict by discussing:

   - Accusing
   - Arguing
   - Attacking (verbally)
   - Blaming
   - Bothering
   - Bullying

- Cheating
- Complaining
- Criticizing
- Embarrassing
- Ignoring
- Joking
- Lying
- Maligning
- Provoking
- Quarreling
- Scolding
- Whining
- Yelling

The items listed above are what tact and diplomacy are sometimes up against. When combinations of them are brought into play, it can be tough to remain cool, calm and tactful, but that is what all family members need to strive for in order to be called champions!

3. The DIPLOMACY GAME involves family members confronting various conflicts and coming up with the right values to deal with them. To be TACTFUL is to cooperate with one another and not be competitive.

Game Rules:

I. The Goal is to move from 1. CRITICAL WORDS to 8. ILL AT EASE.

II. Pennies can be used as movers. Players need to pick pennies with different dates. Pennies with the oldest dates move first.

III. Three (3) sets of the following values will have to written on index cards: CHARACTER, COMMUNICATION, RESPECT, CONFIDENCE, LEADERSHIP, DECISION-MAKING, MORAL COURAGE, RESPONSIBILITY and JUDGMENT. The CHARACTER card is the correct response to all of the problem situations.

IV. Each player draws two cards but must have the correct card to advance from each challenge. See "game board" for the correct value match. In each turn, players discard their cards and draw two (2) new ones. Players holding the correct card may give that card to someone who needs it.

V. Any player who does any of the items listed in #2 above will be disqualified.

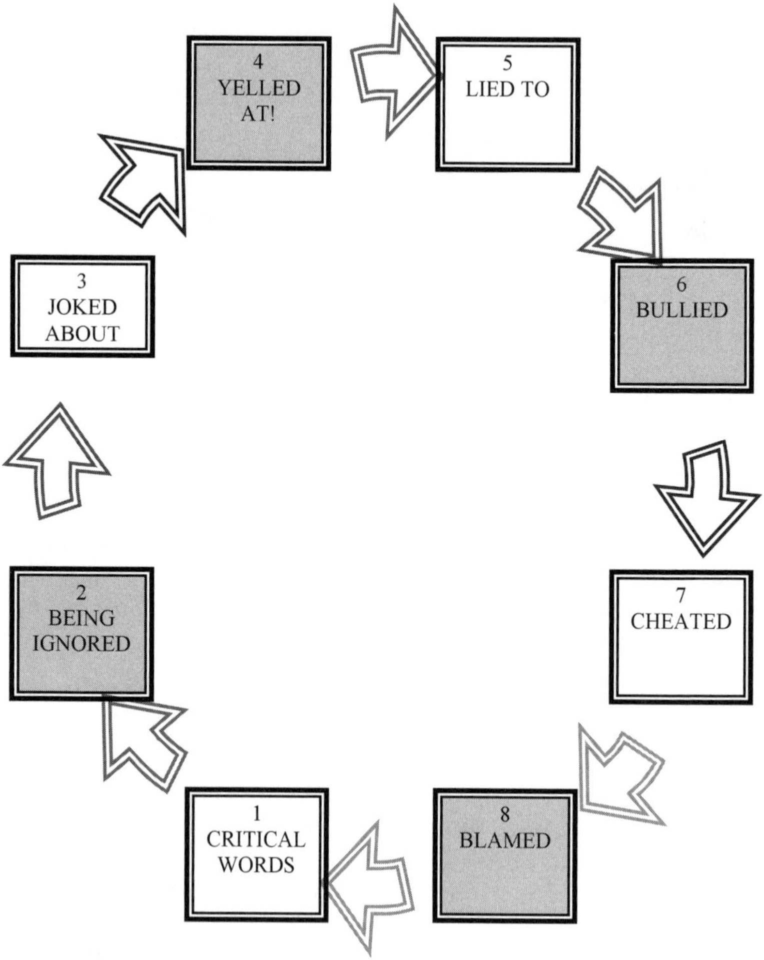

THE DIPLOMACY GAME

1. CHALLENGES	BEST SOLUTION
2. BEING IGNORED	RESPECT
3. JOKED ABOUT	CONFIDENCE
4. YELLED AT!	LEADERSHIP
5. LIED TO	DECISION MAKING
6. BULLIED	MORAL COURAGE
7. CHEATED	RESPONSIBILITY
8. BLAMED	JUDGMENT

CHARACTER

23. Lesson on **TEAMWORK**

TEAMWORK Lesson Objectives:

- Children should write a definition of TEAMWORK.
- Parents will give their children positive verbal reinforcement.

Parents should:

1. Read the introductory summary on TEAMWORK and point out how vital it is for a family to stand together. Team spirit, team play, and team attitude can all be learned in a Championship Family. Explain how all the values, from ABLITY to VIRTUE, are greatly enhanced through teamwork, with all the members of a family playing and working together. If the family is practicing and executing positive values, a virtual powerhouse has been created. Such a "powerhouse family" will find itself winning at home and on the road! Such a family knows that everyone is there for each other!

2. Parent to Child Dialogue (positive verbal reinforcement):

✓ "Let's do this together!"

✓ "Good team play!"

✓ "You guys make a great team!"

✓ "United we soar, divided we sink!"

✓ "Let's win this one for the family!"

✓ "Fantastic job!"

✓ "Come on, time for group hug!"

3. Discuss how unity is a family force multiplier. Together, a family has little to fear but can accomplish so much. Parents need to seek out opportunities for creating family unity and teamwork. Being together does not ensure family teamwork. A game plan is needed and that is

what the Character Parenting Game Plan is all about. For the value lessons, activities and journal entries to have impact, they must done together as a family. Teamwork in the family is essential to reaching all the lesson objectives and outcomes included in this book.

> Parents, tell your children that they are all very important players on the family team. Everyone is needed to execute plays and score points for the family team.
>
> *Coaching Tip*

TEAMWORK

A Championship Family exhibits continuous teamwork as family members play and work together. Doing things together as a family develops and perfects social skills that will empower everyone throughout their lives. This is the one positive value that automatically enhances all the rest of the Core and Life Skill Values. From ABILITY to VIRTUE, they are all made stronger and more lasting through the teamwork of a family. One great person alone can do some interesting things, but a team of great people can do the impossible! Once children learn what teamwork is all about, they will become creative and productive members of many other teams the rest of their lives. Parents have the opportunity to coach their families to greatness!

Pure teamwork is sacrificing and working to support and reinforce the rest of the team. When children see their parents giving up things for them and the family, they sense the deep commitment being made. When children witness their parents bearing any burden and paying any price for them, they feel the love being demonstrated. True family teamwork is deep commitment and love between all the members to the team. A great family does not rest upon the shoulders of just one person—it rests on the collective shoulders of everyone! A Championship Family charges out and takes the playing field together.

❖ **The first team that your child will ever play on is on your family team. The lessons of TEAMWORK learned in the home will forever impact and determine how well they perform on future teams.**

STAND TOGETHER!

> In the family it's not the "I" that's important, it's the "WE."
>
> *Coaching Tip*

TEAMWORK—"The Seven Sticks"
Lesson 44, *McGuffey's Third Eclectic Reader*

THE SEVEN STICKS

1. A man had seven sons who were always quarreling. They left their studies and work to quarrel among themselves. Some bad men were looking forward to the death of their father, to cheat them out of their property by making them quarrel about it.
2. The good old man, one day, called his sons around him. He laid before them seven sticks, which were bound together. He said, "I will pay a hundred dollars to the one who can break this bundle."
3. Each one strained, every nerve to break the bundle. After a long but vain trial, they all said that it could not be done.
4. "And yet, my boys," said the father, "nothing is easier to do." He then untied the bundle and broke the sticks, one by one, with perfect ease.
5. "Ah!" said his sons, "it is easy enough to do it so; anybody could do it in that way."
6. Their father replied, "As it is with these sticks, so it is with you, my sons. So long as you hold fast together and aid each other, you will prosper, and none can injure you."
7. "But if the bond of union is broken, it will happen to you just as it has to these sticks, which lie here broken on the floor."

Questions:
1. Why couldn't the sons break the bundle of sticks but their father could?

2. What lesson was the father teaching his sons?

3. Why does a united group have more power than an individual?

4. Abraham Lincoln once said, "A house divided against itself cannot stand." How can families avoid this problem?

5. What are you doing to strengthen the unity of your family?

CITY DESIGN ACTIVITY

> An architect who puts values into his work is often called a genius. A mother and father who put values into their children are called good parents.
>
> *Coaching Tip*

Children should:
- Relate the core values to a city and family.
- Participate with the family in designing a plan for a city.
- Join the family in the actual building of a city.

❖ **ASSIGNMENT: The family will relate various values to city design, plan their own city and then build it together.**

1. Parents will discuss how cities reflect Core and Life Skill Values just as a family does. Cities are alive with people who exhibit their values and teamwork. Families are alive with its members who show their values and teamwork. Here are discussion points comparing core values in relationship to a city and to a family:

CORE VALUES:

- ☐ **ABILITY**—A city is a reflection of the talents and skills of its people. A family is also a reflection of the talents and skills of its members.
- ☐ **CHARACTER**—A city cannot hide or conceal what it is. A family cannot hide or conceal its true nature.
- ☐ **RESPECT**—A city shows honor and esteem for its history. A family also gives honor to its members and heritage.
- ☐ **CARING**—A city considers the health and safety of its people. A family has a primary mission to protect the health and safety of its members.
- ☐ **FAITH**—A city provides for places and times of worship. A family provides opportunities for its members to worship.
- ☐ **LOVE**—A city bonds itself with its people through form and function. A family forms a tight bond of affection and understanding.
- ☐ **MORAL COURAGE**—A city is made strong by the good deeds of its people. A family is strengthened by the good deeds of its members.
- ☐ **TRUTH**—A city provides justice for its people. A family thrives through the honesty and integrity of its members.
- ☐ **RESPONSIBILITY**—A city prospers when its people do their jobs. A family benefits because its members meet their obligations.
- ☐ **SERVICE**—A city is enhanced when its people help and serve each other. A family shines through its members helping and serving each other.
- ☐ **TACT**—A city is made great through its fairness and tolerance. A family is made great by its own fairness and tolerance.
- ☐ **VIRTUE**—A city is known for its values and earned good reputation. A family is also known for its values and earned good reputation.

It is true that people and cities are not the same, but when you review the values I've discussed, you can see how they uniquely reflect and live an array of values. Both are planned and spontaneous but the value of basic character and virtue does shine through. Certainly, both cities and families rise and fall on the basis of teamwork, exhibited by the people that make them up.

2. **Prior to the actual building of the city, family members will plan exactly what is to be included in their city.** Each family member will be assigned specific structures to work on in at least two of the four main areas. General plans can be sketched out on a piece of paper. Working in pairs is encouraged. Parents will finalize the final assignments. The CITY DESIGN diagram outlines with overlapping circles the general areas of the city:

R—Residential: Housing includes homes and apartments. Schools, local stores, even shopping malls could be included in this area.
G—Government: City hall, college, library, school, police and fire stations are in this category. A monument honoring a person, ideal or event can also be included.
C—Commerce: High-rise office buildings including skyscrapers are in this group. A parking structure, theater, and a restaurant could also be included.
T—Transportation: A portion of a freeway with cars, an airport with planes, and a port facility with ships are included in this category.

Summary of planning requirements:

- The family will act as a **city planning committee** to decide what specific structures will be included in their city design.
- Simple drawings of the proposed structures can also be done. Consider a bulletin board to produce a **master plan** or general idea of what is planned.
- Each family member will need to participate in a minimum of two structures in two different areas.
- Once construction starts all building will be coordinated and approved through the **city planning commissioners** – the parents.
- Every major area, R, G, C, and T, must have at least three structures.
- The city will need to be **named** by the family.
- A **city motto** reflecting the values of the city will need to be agreed upon and written by the family.

3. **Family members will participate in the actual building of their dream city.** While any material can be used, it is recommended that the city be constructed out of LEGO ® bricks, which are a versatile system that can readily produce a city complete with people! A large flat area will need to be designated as the construction site, and if

LEGO elements are used, a substantial quantity of them will need to be purchased. LEGO bricks can be used by the family for years to come for many different construction projects and general enjoyment.

LEGO Nomenclature:

- Bricks—basic LEGO unit which come in a wide variety of configurations and colors.
- Elements—assorted accessories which complement the bricks.
- Mini figures—various people and animals which can bring life to a LEGO environment.
- Robotics—mechanized adaptations of LEGO elements.

City Building Activity:

1. Lay out basic city pattern. Use the CITY DESIGN interlocking circle pattern as a guide.
2. Mark locations for individual construction projects. Names of family members assigned to each location can be written on placards at each site.
3. Assemble LEGO construction materials. Use LEGO mats as a base for each project.
4. Playing of music and serving of refreshments to construction crews is highly encouraged.
5. Event should be captured by photographs showing the progression of the city's construction.
6. City could be built in a day during a planned marathon session.
7. Family members need to give one another both verbal encouragement and praise as their city takes shape.
8. Family members need to actively assist one another during the construction phase.
9. LEGO materials need to be shared. Be sure your supply of them is plentiful.
10. If the first session is not enough time, plan another one.
11. Celebrate the city's completion. Spend time examining the city in every detail. Take more pictures!
12. Above all else, make sure that everyone has a great time. Remember this is a TEAMWORK activity where the entire family works and plays together.

CITY DESIGN

R—Residential G—Government

C—Commerce T—Transportation

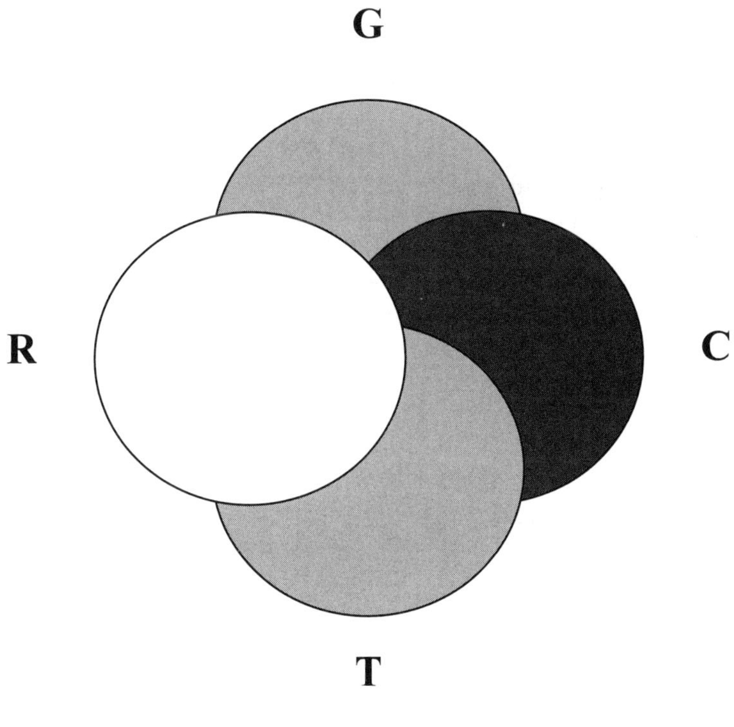

24. Lesson on **VIRTUE**

VIRTUE Lesson Objectives:
- Children will write a definition of VIRTUE.
- Parents will give their children positive verbal reinforcement.

Parents should:
1. Read the introductory summary on VIRTUE and explain how all the values are present in this final value. Being good is not only following the Core Values, but also practicing the Life Skill Values as well. Moral and positive values compliment each other making all of us the very best we can be. Virtue is not a final destination but a summit we are trying to scale throughout life. This final value gives us the direction we need as every day comes and goes.

2. Parent to Child Dialogue (positive verbal reinforcement):

✓ "You should be proud of yourself."

✓ "You're a pleasure to have in the family."

✓ "You walk the talk."

✓ 'You are very good."

✓ "You're my shining star!"

✓ "Your compass is pointing the right way."

✓ "You are a good person."

3. VIRTUE and CHARACTER are the essential values of the Championship Family. They are the ingredients of a good and satisfying life.

> Parents, center your drill and practices around VIRTUE and CHARACTER as you coach and teach your children. They will forever be ready and willing to succeed in life.
>
> *Coaching Tip*

VIRTUE

There is no substitute for virtue; a family must have a core of moral values. Coaching a child to develop moral awareness and ethical reasoning is critical to their knowing right from wrong and having the moral courage to do what is right. At an early age, children need to practice effective moral conduct that will become a habit for their entire life. Moral compasses can steer us through severe storms while moral anchors will steady us in times of uncertainty and doubt. Parents have the responsibility of faithfully setting the moral compasses of their children. Neglecting to do this is setting children adrift at the mercy of the shifting and hostile currents of an indifferent world.

Virtue needs to be visible and active in the family. Parents must model virtuous behavior so their children can experience its presence and power. Virtue is not just an idea; it is a practice that governs our thoughts and actions. Parents cannot shrink from virtue—they must become its champion. Once practiced on a continuous basis, virtue becomes the rule, not the exception. Family members need to know that virtue is the only pathway open to the truly good life. Virtue enables us to stand tall against adversity and allows us to reach the summit of all values. A Championship Family cannot win unless virtue is within its members and practiced faithfully.

❖ **Virtue is the essence of your character. It is the blueprint of your true behavior and the roadmap for your daily actions—it is the inspirational mountain peak of your life's journey.**

BE GOOD!

> Virtue is the mighty fortress of the family. It is where you make your first and last stand. It is your best protection and finest hour.
>
> *Coaching Tip*

VIRTUE—"If I Were a Sunbeam"
Lesson 13, *McGuffey's Second Eclectic Reader*

IF I WERE A SUNBEAM
1. If I were a sunbeam,
I know what I'd do;
I would seek white lilies,
Roaming woodlands through.
I would steal among them,
Softest light I'd shed,
Until every lily
Raised its drooping head.

VIRTUE—Questions:
1. How do you show your virtue?

2. Describe your own sunbeam—those traits that make you both positive and enthusiastic.

3. How bright is your sunbeam?

4. How is your moral excellence growing every day?

5. Are you faithfully following your moral compass? Where is it taking you?

"STAND"
The Freedom's Writers Diary

"Don't be afraid to be what you are,
'cause all you can be, is you!
You'll never be anything else but you,
so be the best you, you can be."

VIRTUE—Questions:
1. Is being "proud" a virtue?

2. Are you "standing up" for yourself?

3. Are you being the best you can be? How?

4. Is being good important to you? Why?

5. How do you know that you are a good person? Explain.

MORAL COMPASS ACTIVITY

Set the family compass on the true North of Character and point your East setting toward Virtue; with the West pointing at the other Core Values, and the South pointing to the Life Skill Values.

Coaching Tip

Children should:

- Rank the Life Skill Values explaining how they use them in daily activities.
- Rank the Core Values explaining how they influence their daily actions.
- Design and make a Moral Compass using all 24 values.

❖ **ASSIGNMENT: Children discuss their rank ordering of the Life Skill and Core Values with their parents and make their own Moral Compass.**

1. **Children rank the LIFE SKILL VALUES from 1 to 12, starting with the most important.** Each value should be reviewed and discussed with a parent. How does the value work for them in their daily activities? Is the value useful and productive? The following Life Skill Value listing is alphabetical:

COMMUNICATION
CONFIDENCE
CREATIVITY
DECISION MAKING
FITNESS
JUDGMENT
KNOWLEDGE
LEADERSHIP
MOTIVATION
ORGANIZATION
PERSEVERANCE
TEAMWORK

Children should write a brief explanation of how the value can be used in their daily activities. They can also describe how each value can make valuable contributions to a successful living. These Life Skill Values all contribute to positive outcomes and are the basic ingredients to success and achievement.

2. **Children rank the CORE VALUES from 1 to 12, starting with the most important.** It should be fairly apparent that CHARACTER and VIRTUE are very important, but the actual ranking is up to each child. Again, the ranking of each value is accompanied with an explanation of exactly how they are best demonstrated and exhibited. Parents will assist their children as they complete the ranking and write brief statements as to how these values influence their daily actions.

ABILITY
CARING
CHARACTER
FAITH
LOVE
MORAL COURAGE
RESPONSIBILITY
RESPECT
SERVICE
TACT
TRUTH
VIRTUE

Children can explain how each value contributes to making a person all they can be. **Character** is really having the resolve to exhibit the Core and Life Skill Values consistently. **Virtue** is the faithful practicing of these same values, thereby becoming a truly "good" person. You cannot have one without the other. In other words, CHARACTER is practicing all the values while VIRTUE is the development and perfection of these same values.

3. **Using the Moral Compass template as a guide, children will complete their own compass.** While the North and East settings are already established, children will select their top Core Value other than Character and Virtue for the West setting. For the South compass setting, children will select their top Life Skill value. The compass will need to be drawn and colored with the four values prominently written.

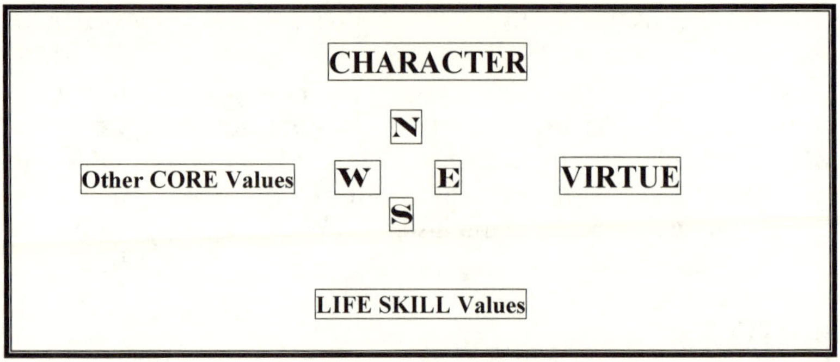
CHARACTER
N
Other CORE Values
W
E
VIRTUE
S
LIFE SKILL Values

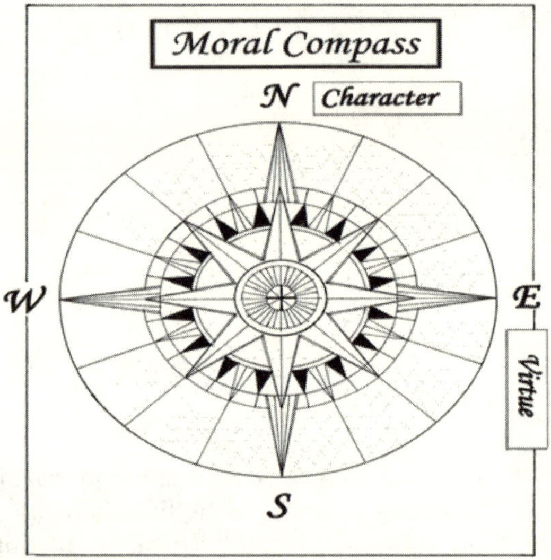
Moral Compass
N
Character
W
E
Virtue
S

JOURNAL: CELEBRATIONS

A Championship Family takes time to celebrate major events and accomplishments. A family needs to celebrate as a team of very special people. Chronicle the moments and memories that have defined your family. Above all else—celebrate the people and what they do!

FAMILY **BIRTHDAYS**

FAMILY **AWARDS and ACHIEVEMENTS**

FAMILY **WEDDINGS**

FAMILY **VICTORIES and SPECIAL DAYS**

FAMILY **ART and POETRY**

FAMILY BIRTHDAYS

Journal Assignment: Family members will write newspaper-style articles about another member's birthday. Parents can help their children write them. Articles need to be written as if newspaper reporters were covering the birthday for local papers. Photos can be included, and a photo of the person blowing out his or her candles is very appropriate. Look at newspaper articles to get ideas for style and organization.

Everyone's birthday needs to be celebrated in some way. Refer to the birthday celebration list below. Cards and gifts are encouraged. Homemade cards are fun. Remember, it is not the cost of the gift that makes it special. Family members can collaborate on this by giving a combined gift and/or planning a special outing.

No birthday is really complete without a cake and candles. The exact number of candles to indicate the total years being celebrated is not necessary. Families need to make the observance of birthdays a "big deal." Usually, kids will want to invite some of their friends.

Birthday Celebration Idea List:

- Party at home
- Party at home and movie
- Party in the garage
- Slumber party
- BBQ in the backyard or front yard
- Pool party (requires a swimming pool)
- Party at the grandparents
- Party in the park
- Party at a lake
- Party in the snow (if available)
- Beach party
- Restaurant setting
- Amusement park setting
- Theater setting
- Surprise party!
- Bowling party

FAMILY AWARDS and ACHIEVEMENT

Journal Assignment: Family members will write newspaper-style articles about another member's award or accomplishment. Parents can assist with this project. Articles need to be written as if newspaper reporters were covering the special accomplishment. Photos can be included. Look at newspaper articles to get ideas for style and organization.

Awards and accomplishments can range from Noble Prizes to class awards for attendance. Any kind of academic, work, athletic, or creative arts recognition should be reported on. Parents are encouraged to institute their own family awards to reward good performance. Special award certificates can be prepared to honor those receiving family awards. An awards "banquet" could be held to recognize several family members for their accomplishments. Refer to the family awards idea list below.

No individual accomplishment or dedication to work by a family member should go unnoticed. Awards and accomplishments need to be properly noted and celebrated. That one special recognition can help motivate children to continue to excel in an area or try to achieve in others.

Family Awards Idea List:

- Hero Award (Random act of kindness)
- Character Award (Display of character value)
- MVP Award (All around family service)
- Home Improvement Badge (Work around the house)
- Landscape Badge (Yard work)
- Purple Heart (Bravery handling an injury)
- Positive Attitude Award (Enthusiastic family service)
- Scholarship Golden Star Award (Excellence in school)
- Meritorious Service Award (Community service)
- Parent's Award (Series of accomplishments)
- Reader's Certificate (Reading fifty books)
- Literary Prize Award (Achievement in literature)
- Artist's Ribbon (Achievement in art)
- Mathematics Star Award (Achievement in math)
- Science Star Award (Achievement in science)

FAMILY WEDDINGS

Journal Assignment: Family members will write newspaper-style articles about their parents' and grandparents' weddings. Parents can help their children write articles. Articles need to be written as if newspapers were covering the weddings. Photos for the events are essential. Look at newspaper articles for style and organization ideas.

The articles will require research into family history. Questions need to be asked concerning the myriad of details that concern any wedding. Consider the weddings' date, location, ceremony details, people attending, gifts, photos, any memorabilia, and honeymoon information. See family wedding question list.

While family weddings survive in old photos or albums, the writing of newspaper articles will reveal some facts and information previously unknown. The wedding articles will all go into the FAMILY JOURNAL for current and future generations.

Family Wedding Question List:

- Who got married, when, and where?
- How old were the bride and groom?

- Were they working or going to school?
- Where did the wedding take place?
- Is there a wedding program?
- Who officiated at the wedding?
- Who made up the wedding party (best man, maid of honor, ushers, bridesmaids)?
- Are there photos or film recordings of the wedding?
- Is there a list of who attended the wedding?
- Is there a record of wedding gifts?
- Is there a newspaper article on the wedding?
- What does the married couple remember? First home?
- Where did they go for a honeymoon? Are there pictures?
- Are there any recollections from other people?

FAMILY VICTORIES and SPECIAL DAYS

Journal Assignment: Family members will write newspaper-style articles about another member's "victory" or special day. Parents can help their children write articles. They need to be written as if outside sources were reporting the special event for the local papers. Photos can be included. Look at newspaper articles to get ideas for style and organization.

A "victory" can take many different forms—from learning how to ride a bicycle for the first time to being promoted to advancing another grade level at school. For parents, a "victory" could be buying a new a car, receiving a promotion, or being recognized in the community. A "Special Day" for a child could be their first day at school, whereas for a parent, it could be an anniversary or receiving some good news. See family victory and special day list below.

A family thrives on victories and special days. They help energize and motivate everyone. That is why these events need to be recorded and remembered. Sometimes a victory passes by quickly without receiving the notice and recognition that it deserves.

Family Victory and Special Day List:
- Learning how to do something for the first time
- Solving a tough problem

- Winning something
- Receiving an award
- Becoming part of a team or group
- Winning on a sports team
- Overcoming an adversity
- Being promoted at school or work
- Meeting someone special
- Going someplace special
- Giving a special performance
- Doing something that was difficult
- Completing a major project
- Beating the odds!
- Coming from behind to win!

FAMILY ART and POETRY

Journal Assignment: Family members will write newspaper-style articles on another member's art and poetry entry in the family art and poetry show. Parents can help their children with this project. Articles need to be written as if newspaper reporters were covering the show. Photos should be included. Look at newspaper articles to get ideas for style and organization.

Family members will have to complete artwork in any form (pencil, crayon, ink, pastel, watercolor, oils, photography, collage, tiles, wood, or metal) and any style. Family members will each write a poem on any topic using any style. Parents will assist their kids in completing these two projects. Once completed, the artwork and poems will be displayed in a family show. All items will receive certificate awards. A reception will be held for the show with program and awards dinner. Articles will include full descriptions of each family member's entries along with a photo of them. The show and dinner will also be mentioned. See family art and poetry show categories and awards below.

A family needs a chance to let its members create art and poetry, and share it among themselves. The art and poetry show will not only result in news articles, but in works that can be displayed in the home. The artistic endeavors of all family members should be encouraged.

Family Art and Poetry Show Categories:

- Original art any media
- Photography
- Collage
- Other media: tile, wood, metal
- Poems of any type
- Poems that tell a story
- Poems about people

Family Art and Poetry Show Awards:

- Certificate of achievement (everyone)
- Best art entry (each category)
- Best poem entry (each category)
- Best of show (family members vote—ties okay)

NEWS REPORT FORMAT

HEADLINE: ______________________________

Date: ______________________________

City & State: ______________________________

Reporter: ______________________________

Include an action shot

Include a caption explaining the photograph and the name of the photographer.

CHAPTER FIVE

CHAMPIONSHIP SEASONS:
(Life Satisfaction)

The culmination of the CHARACTER PARENTING GAME PLAN is having Championship Seasons. This is the family realizing the power of a value driven life with parents actively coaching their children in achieving values. Such winning seasons exhibit the life satisfaction practices of Soaring, Imagining, Pursuing, Creating and Thriving. CHAMPIONSHIP SEASONS is where parents and children can:

- **SOAR**—CLIMBING SWIFTLY, RISING ABOVE THE ORDINARY
- **IMAGINE**—DREAMING OF WHAT COULD BE, BOLDLY GOING OVER THE HORIZON
- **PURSUE**—STRIVING TO ACHIEVE OR ACCOMPLISH, ADVANCING RELENTLESSLY
- **CREATE**—PRODUCING THROUGH SELF-EFFORT, BRINGING INTO EXISTENCE
- **THRIVE**—FLOURISHING WITH PURPOSE AND ENERGY, SELF-ACTUALIZING

PARENTS' CHAMPIONSHIP FAMILY GUIDE:

✓ Vision & Mission
✓ Parenting Good Habits
✓ GAME PLAN Notes

SOAR

CLIMBING SWIFTLY,
RISING ABOVE THE ORDINARY

SOAR is to

amplify,

arise,

ascend,

augment,

boost,

build,

climb,

expand,

extend,

grow,

lift,

increase,

multiply,

rise,

and skyrocket!

Parents, connect your children to these thoughts and actions, thereby making them habits in their daily walk.

Coaching Tip

IMAGINE

DREAMING OF WHAT COULD BE,
Boldly going OVER THE HORIZON.

IMAGINE is to

assume,

believe,

conceive,

dream up,

envisage,

envision,

fancy,

fantasize,

foresee,

infer,

picture,

presume,

suppose,

visualize,

and stargaze!

Parents, connect your children to these thoughts and actions, thereby making them habits in their daily walk.

Coaching Tip

PURSUE

STRIVING
TO ACHIEVE OR ACCOMPLISH,
ADVANCING RELENTLESSLY

PURSUE is to

aim for,

aspire to,

be after,

be intent upon,

chase,

give chase,

go after,

push forward,

run after,

seek,

strive for,

surge,

track,

trail,

and try, try, try again!

Parents, connect your children to these thoughts and actions, thereby making them habits in their daily walk.

Coaching Tip

CREATE

PRODUCING
THROUGH SELF-EFFORT,
BRINGING INTO EXISTENCE

CREATE is to

bring into being,

cause,

concoct,

construct,

contrive,

design,

develop,

devise,

fabricate,

fashion,

form,

format,

make,

invent,

and originate!

Parents, connect your children to these thoughts and actions, thereby making them habits in their daily walk.

Coaching Tip

COZY LOG HOME QUILT BLOCK

Fabric needed for the Cozy Log Home quilt block:

1 fat quarter:	Dark or Medium Brown (logs)
Small pieces of:	Light Blue (sky)
	Soft Yellow/Gold (windows)
	Dark Red (door & chimney)
	Medium Green (grass)
	Dark Green (roof)

Wash, dry and press all fabric prior to cutting.

Cut the following pieces of fabric:

Brown	1 1/2" x 8 1/2" (5)	***Yellow/Gold***	1 1/2" x 2 1/2" (5)
	1 1/2" x 1 1/2" (10)	***Dark Red***	2 1/2" x 4 1/2" (1)
	1 1/2" x 1 1/4" (8)		1 1/2" x 1 1/2" (1)
	1 1/4" x 1 1/4" (2)	***Medium Green***	1 3/4" x 8 1/2" (1)
Light Blue	1 1/2" x 4 1/4" (1)	***Dark Green***	2 3/4" x 8 1/2" (1)
	1 1/2" x 3 1/4" (1)		
	2 3/4" x 2 3/4" (2)		

Quilt Block directions:

- **Use 1/4" seams throughout.**
- **Press each seam after stitching.**

1. Stitch four 1 1/2" x 1 1/2" pieces of brown fabric to each other, to make the section on the left side of the door.

2. Stitch this four-piece section to the longer side of the red door.

3. Stitch two 1 1/2" x 1 1/2" pieces of brown fabric together. Do this three times, making log sections on either side of the lower windows.

4. Stitch this two-piece brown fabric to either long side of the yellow window fabric. Repeat for the second lower window.

5. Stitch the two 1 1/2" x 5 1/2" brown pieces together lengthwise.

6. Stitch this section onto the lower side of the section with windows.

7. Stitch this window section onto the door section (see above).

8. Stitch two 1 1/2" x 1 3/4" pieces of brown together to form a wall section for the upper floor. (Stitch the 1 3/4" sides together.) Repeat this three more times.

9. Stitch the yellow/gold windows between the four wall sections.

10. Stitch three 1 1/2" x 8 1/2" brown pieces together lengthwise.

11. Stitch this section to the bottom edge of the just-completed window section.

12. Stitch two 1 1/8" x 8 1/2" brown pieces together lengthwise.

13. Stitch this wall section to the top edge of the just-completed window section.

14. Stitch this whole upper floor section to the lower floor section.

15. Stitch one 2 3/4" x 2 3/4" piece of blue fabric to one end of the 2 3/4" x 8 1/2" dark green fabric. Stitch diagonally from the lower corner of the dark green fabric to the opposite corner of the blue fabric. After stitching, cut 1/4" from the seam on the outside of the seam. Flip the blue fabric over to form the part of the sky on the left side of the roof. Repeat this at the right end of the roof.

16. Stitch the 1 1/2" x 4 3/4" piece of blue fabric to the 1 1/2" x 1 1/2" piece of red fabric. Stitch the piece of blue to the other side of the red fabric.

17. Stitch this section to the top of the roof.

18. Stitch the bottom edge of the roof section to the top edge of the upper floor section.

19. Stitch the 1 3/4" x 8 1/2" piece of medium green to the bottom edge of the door and wall section.

Kaye Dehrer

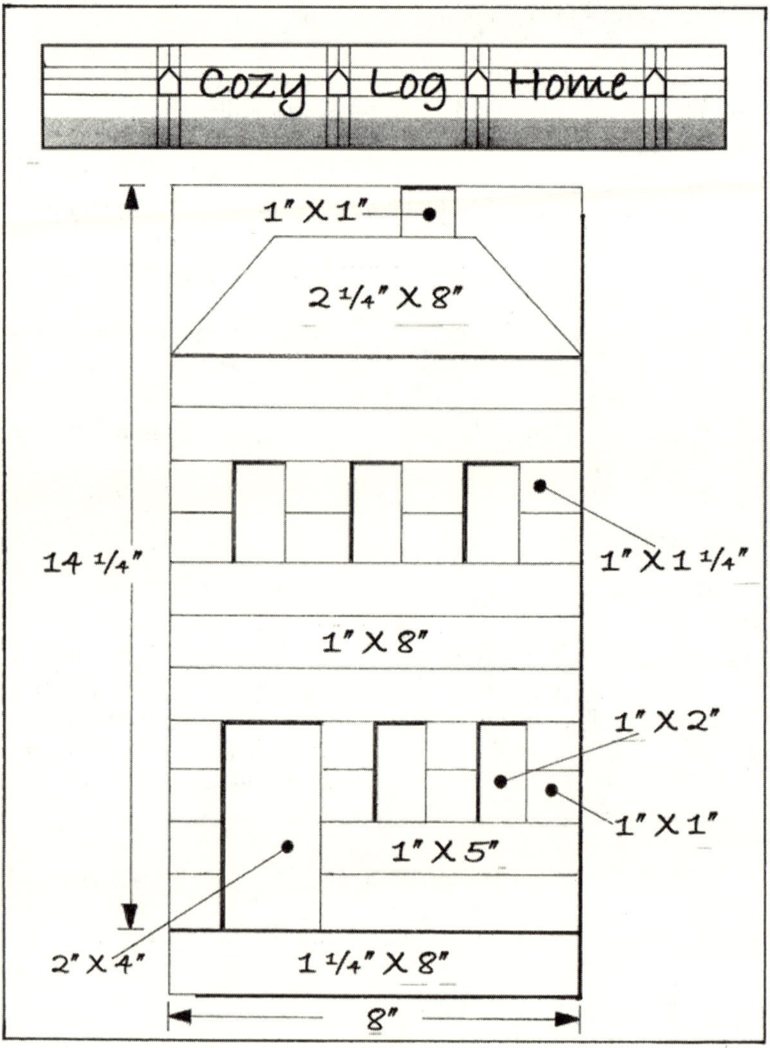
Cozy Log Home
1" X 1"
2 1/4" X 8"
1" X 1 1/4"
14 1/4"
1" X 8"
1" X 2"
1" X 1"
1" X 5"
2" X 4"
1 1/4" X 8"
8"

THRIVE

FLOURISHING
WITH PURPOSE AND ENERGY,
SELF-ACTUALIZING

THRIVE is to

be fortunate,

be successful,

blossom,

boom,

burgeon,

fatten,

flourish,

get ahead,

get on,

grow rich,

grow vigorously,

live enthusiastically,

prosper,

succeed,

and turn out well!

Parents, connect your children to these thoughts and actions, thereby making them habits in their daily walk.

Coaching Tip

AGE of DISCOVERY

The shoreline of the familiar and known swiftly disappears as the passage of time draws you to distant and unexpected destinations. The winds and currents endlessly twist and turn us.

I
Challenges lift you above the ordinary to do the exceptional.

Ability provides the resources to be the person you were meant to be, leaving behind amazing footprints.

Character enables you to set a good example and astound others with your values and presence.

Motivation lights your fire!

Perseverance is the powerful wind at your back and the single greatest reason you will ultimately prevail.

Respect is your resolve to give and to receive esteem.

II
Adversity can surprise you with the thought that life can be unfair.

Caring illuminates your heroic kindness.

Creativity is seeing what is not visible.

Faith causes you to trust in God knowing that your life has both purpose and destiny.

Fitness allows you renew and sustain yourself.

Love serves as your most magnificent engine and the wellspring of miracles.

Moral Courage is your resolve beyond the physical measure.

Truth defines your inner integrity and accountability as a person.

III
Difficulties are the pain of yesterday, the lesson of today, and the memory of tomorrow.

Communication is your greatest interpersonal tool and persuader.

Confidence manifests itself as an irresistible force!

Judgment is knowing what is right and then doing it.

Knowledge is the true measure of your reach, your heartfelt satisfaction, your highest standard and your brightest sky.

Responsibility is your brave commitment to always try and make no excuses.

IV
Defeats are common, but rising above them is uncommon.

Decision Making must be consistent and value driven.

Leadership tells others that you are someone worthy of following and trusting.

Organization is your plan and preparation for success.

Service above self is your greatest triumph.

Tact is being a sensitive and considerate person.

Teamwork multiplies your individual worth by clearing the deck for extraordinary things to happen.

Virtue is your shining paradigm for personal excellence, your moral high ground, your steady compass and your safe passage as you venture boldly over the horizon.

V
Hope rises as an assured and certain promise that you will forever Soar, Imagine, Pursue, Create and Thrive!

As your own vessel cuts through calm and stormy seas,
your **AGE of DISCOVERY** continues unabated with the rise
and fall of the endless ocean of time.

Gary Dehrer

A Worthy Goal

The mentor and the student sat down at their usual table in the café and, as usual, the mentor ordered a cup of coffee and the student ordered a donut. Twice a month, the two would meet in the morning to discuss a topic selected by the mentor.

After the waiter served the coffee and donut, the mentor commenced the discussion as he always did with a brief introduction. "Pursue. That is the topic we have been discussing in our last couple of meetings. Now let's see here. The time before last we concluded that we must be proactive and pursue things instead of sitting idly by and allowing unwanted things to pursue us. Then, last time, we concluded that some goals are worthy of our pursuit and others are not. As a result of those conclusions, if I remember correctly, you chose a worthy and most noble goal to pursue. Which leads me to the question we must consider this time: how is your pursuit going?"

The student fidgeted nervously in his chair and quickly swallowed a bite of donut before answering. "Well, you see sir, I have decided not to pursue that goal any longer. I carefully followed a plan of action, but despite my best efforts the goal seems to be impossible. So, I think I'll move on and try something else."

The mentor was not surprised by this development, but he decided to act surprised to prove his point. "Really? After a couple of weeks, you are abandoning your goal?"

"Don't get me wrong," the student replied, feeling suddenly defensive. "I did try, but it was frustrating. I suffered a number of setbacks and realized the goal simply cannot be achieved. Not by me, anyways."

The mentor sipped his coffee slowly, quietly, allowing the student to continue to shift uncomfortably in his chair. Then, lowering his cup to his chin, the mentor said, "I see. I can accept that decision, but I would suggest that the next time you decide to pursue a worthy objective that you actually PURSUE it."

The response was too much for the student. "Sir, perhaps you didn't hear me," he said impatiently. "I followed several steps to accomplish that goal. When those steps didn't work, I tried some others. Every time, though, I was met with defeat. I did PURSUE it."

The mentor paused thoughtfully and placed his coffee cup on its saucer. "If you truly pursue something, then the pursuit does not stop until you have it. So long as the goal is worthy and the decision to pursue it has been made carefully, then the pursuit must continue until the goal is accomplished."

"Do you mean to say that if I pursued that goal for fifty years and did not achieve it, I should go on pursuing it?" the student asked, astonished.

"That is correct, young man."

"But sir, if the goal is clearly futile, wouldn't that be a waste of time?"

"Absolutely not," the mentor replied. "A worthy goal is never a waste of time."

The student was amazed at these statements and thought to himself that surely his mentor was wrong this time. "Sir, have you ever pursued a goal that seemed impossible to attain and led to a great deal of frustration?"

"Yes."

Pleased with the mentor's admission, the student decided to see if he could trap the mentor. "And I am sure that you tried several different things, none of which were immediately successful. Is that correct?"

"Indeed it is."

The student was in his element now, victoriously chomping on his donut as he spoke. "And did you ever think about quitting the pursuit and giving up the goal?"

"I must admit that I did," the mentor said. "Several times."

"So, I bet you stopped pursuing that goal, didn't you," the student quipped as he savored the last bite of his donut.

"No, I did not stop. I continue pursuing it to this day."

"Well then," said the student, disappointed, "would you mind telling me what this goal is?"

"I don't mind at all," the mentor replied patiently. "The seemingly impossible, frustrating, and yet worthy goal that I will not stop pursuing is YOU."

Stephen Dehrer

Passenger

Time has passed, left me,
trapping the image
of a tiny voice
asking once again,
pulling with a small hand
at my sleeve
till I am at her level,
hot breath against my face.
A flood of thought,
a moment,
when we traveled
in a green van,
tires passing over the same road,
adding a footprint,
a place where the branch broke.
When we passed by,
Maybe I didn't look close enough,
But she did, and she will tell you.
If you listen, if you're open
and let her stargaze.
She will remind you
that we have to wake up
sometimes,
to catch those dreams.
I could catch a lot
with these large hands
if we got out
and walked,
slowed it down
long enough—
to blow out the thistle,
walk barefoot in wet grass,
let her point out each star,
then use them to guide us home.
As we travel
in a green van
not just down a road,
but down a vein that pulses,
with each beat of the heart.

Janet Dehrer-Bertrand

Seeking Shelter

I wake to the sound of wild horses
taking shelter against the old barn,
hooves scraping the ground.
My sisters and I lay in bed,
I'm in the middle,
Ma's quilts heavy on me.
I wonder if she's warm downstairs,
or hissing at Pa to keep his cold feet
over on his side of the bed.
I want to creep toward the window
with my lantern to see
the horses' manes flying,
but my feet would have to touch
the cold, wood floor.
My sister Bonnie is never afraid like me,
in her thick, blond braids and torn jeans
squishing a spider in the closet.
I saw her do it once—
with only her bare foot.

In the fading darkness,
I dream in grey and purple-
I'm out on the prairie,
pulling myself up
on an ivory-maned horse
and it streaks out across the snow-
white under flecks of flame
suspended in black gel.
The quiet night touches me gently
tucking in around me.
The stars never complain,
never resent me,
shifting in their seats.
Fixed in darkness, they watch me ride
like Joan of Arc on her steed,
steel lance dividing the air
into symmetry
as I lead the way to Orleone.

I want to see all the falling stars
and not miss a single one.
Those that fall to earth
without a wish
are lost forever,
a tremor along the ground
before they finally collapse in the snow.
My horse and I fly,
riding above the clouds,
my lantern far behind.
I'm not a girl anymore,
but a warrior.
I can ride across Montana in my bare feet,
not even cold enough to seek shelter.

Nancy Dobson

INDEX OF A CHAMPIONSHIP FAMILY

CHAMPIONSHIP SEASONS (Life Satisfaction)—See Chapter Five
Any family that practices the 24 Core and Life Skill values in their daily life will become *winners* as they experience *soaring, imagining, pursuing, creating,* and *thriving.*

CHARACTER (Core Value)—See Lesson 2
It's all about having values, conscience, and courage; your good character towers over any other accomplishments. Without character, there is really nothing left.

CHARACTER PARENTING—See GAME PLAN
This is parents coaching their children in developing lifelong habits of character through the 24 Core and Life Skill values. This is parents actively teaching values to their kids.

CHARACTER TOWER (Activity)—See Lesson 2
The "Six Pillars of Character" including *trustworthiness, respect, responsibility, fairness, caring,* and *citizenship* form the framework of our own "towers." Such a tower can never fall.

CITY DESIGN (Activity)—See Lesson 23
The Core Values are integral to cities as well as people. Architects and parents who understand this will plan and help build great works. Values expand and excel through teamwork.

CLUTTER FREE (Activity)—See Lesson 20
Organization of the material possessions and our minds greatly increases our efficiency to live value driven lives. To organize is to get ready for success.

COACHING TIPS
Parents as coaches must focus on the means to build character and how to measure desired outcomes. Kids are highly trainable in the early years of their development.

COMMUNICATION (Life Skill)—See Lesson 13
A parent who is a good listener, is a good communicator. Use communication as a tool of *motivation, reinforcement,* and *understanding.* Great communicators are winners.

CONDITIONING (Strengths)—See Chapter Two
Strengths including CARING, CREATIVITY, FAITH, FITNESS, LOVE, MORAL COURAGE, and TRUTH provide *force projection* for CHARACTER. *Character through strength.*

CONFIDENCE (Life Skill)—See Lesson 14
Kids will not believe in themselves unless their parents do. To believe in your kids will help build their confidence thereby increasing their chances at living successful lives.

CORE VALUES—See Lessons 1, 2, 5, 6, 8, 10, 11, 12, 17, 21, 22, and 24
These personal values include: ABILITY, CHARACTER, RESPECT, CARING, FAITH, LOVE, MORAL COURAGE, TRUTH, RESPONSIBILITY, SERVICE, TACT, and VIRTUE.

CREATE (Life Satisfaction)—See Chapter Five: SOAR to THRIVE
Parents need to connect their kids to the mindset of "PRODUCING THROUGH SELF-EFFORT, BRINGING INTO EXISTENCE." This is an important part of life satisfaction.

CREATIVITY (Life Skill)—See Lesson 7
Families cannot achieve the incredible unless they can visualize and feel it first. Being creative is within all of us but we must reach for it and venture out of our comfort zone to embrace it.

D

DECISION MAKING (Life Skill)—See Lesson 18
Making good choices is a lifelong challenge but kids who learn early how to make value driven choices have acquired a valuable skill that will forever enhance their lives.

DIPLOMACY GAME (Activity)—See Lesson 22
Tactful interpersonal relationships will yield satisfying outcomes. Difficult people and situations can be overcome through effective application of Core and Life Skill values.

DISCIPLINE—See Lessons 1 through 24
Character value training results in the building of strong discipline in children. Kids who are in control of their emotions have been freed to live purposeful and productive lives.

E

EDUCATION—See Lessons 1 through 24. See also Chapter Five
The greatest natural resource of America is its youth. Character education is the prerequisite for achieving our nation's educational agenda of a highly literate and qualified workforce.

F

FAITH (Core Value)—See Lesson 8
Championship Families find their greatest strength in the word of God. There is simply no substitute for having a strong faith and families without this are at great risk.

FAMILY ACTION PLAN (Activity)—See Lesson 4
Putting a man on the moon required a plan and so does getting things done in the family. Family action plans can make unbelievable things happen but everyone must participate.

FAMILY JOURNAL—See INTRODUCTIONS, LIFESTYLE, GREATEST STORIES, and CELEBRATIONS
Family participation in putting together a Family Journal will help join everyone together while creating a lasting chronicle of your time together. Memories are the ties that bind.

FAMILY NEWSLETTER (Activity)—See Lesson 13
Family members gain a sense of togetherness through interaction and sharing. The key is to be interested in one another and writing a family newsletter can achieve this special bonding.

FAMILY OF READERS (Activity)—See Lesson ?
The greatest learning tool a child can have is the ability to read. A family that reads together will enjoy satisfaction and success. A life without books is truly impoverished.

FAMILY TRADITIONS (Activity)—See Lesson 10
The soul of a family can be found in its traditions and customs which mirror the love and caring that is present. A family without traditions are really strangers sharing the same house.

FAMILY VALUES—See Lesson 24
A family needs direction and purpose provided by the Core and Life Skill values to properly set their moral compass. Value driven families are *Championship Families.*

FRIENDSHIP CHECKLIST (Activity)—See Lesson 5
The important thing is to have friends that share your belief in moral and positive values. Good friendships are built upon mutual trust and truth not deception and manipulation.

FITNESS (Life Skill)—See Lesson 9
Proper rest, nutrition, and exercise energize and power Championship Families. Strong characters are compromised in weak bodies. Healthy kids have the best chance to be winners.

FIVE QUESTIONS (Activity)—See Lesson 12
Family members must pledge themselves to be *truth seekers* thereby building their integrity and mutual respect. Truth is absolute in the Championship Family.

FIVE TESTS (Activity)—See Lesson 15
Making ethical judgments rests on the ability to carefully consider values and not rush to hasty choices. Kids have to learn to think things through on their own and make the tough calls.

G

GAME PLAN
Good parent coaches have to have a Game Plan to get their families on a winning course. Character Parenting is essentially providing effective character training for children.

GAME TIME (Life Skills)—See Chapter Four
Life skills including DECISION MAKING, LEADERSHIP, ORGANIZATION, SERVICE, TACT, TEAMWORK, and VIRTUE provide the tools for families to win.

GREATEST PRESIDENTS (Activity)—See Lesson 19
American Presidential greatness can be measured in terms of values; parents are in a never ending pursuit of leadership excellence and as such are an enduring role model.

GREATEST STORIES—See FAMILY JOURNAL
Every family has its own special narrative that needs to be told and recorded through STORYTELLING, SHORT STORIES and HISTORY assignments.

H

HARMONY
Peace in the family just doesn't happen, it is the result of family members who value each other and look forward to sharing their time together. Growing together is a key outcome.

HAVING FUN—See FAMILY JOURNAL and Lessons 1 through 24
The whole idea of a Championship Family is to have fun learning and growing together. Laughter in the family should be heard a lot as parents and kids enjoy one another.

I

IMAGINE (Life Satisfaction)—See Chapter Five: SOAR to THRIVE
Parents need to connect their kids to the mindset of "DREAMING OF WHAT COULD BE, BOLDLY GOING OVER THE HORIZON." This is an important part of life satisfaction.

INTERACTION—See CHAMPIONSHIP FAMILY—CHARACTER PARENTING Book
A critical component of this book is parents spending quality time with their children. Nothing can take the place of a parent being there for their kids; this makes the greatest of differences.

INTRODUCTIONS—See FAMILY JOURNAL
A family needs to get to know one another and be formally introduced developing a sense of togetherness and specialty. Don't have a family Coat of Arms, then design one!

NEW INVENTION (Activity)—See Lesson 7
Family members need to challenge themselves to see what is not there and to dream of things that never were and to create them. Living is daily application and transfer of knowledge.

J

JOURNAL—See FAMILY JOURNAL
The concept of a collaborative family journal is to draw family members together in creating a chronicle that otherwise would not have been created. The journal will mirror your family.

JUDGMENT (Life Skill)—See Lesson 15
Making good judgment calls is where Championship Families truly *stand and deliver.* Good choices always consider the consequences. Everyone needs to know when to say, no.

K

KIDS—See MESSAGE to KIDS
This entire book is about how to provide meaningful character education for kids. Acquiring Core and Life Skill values in the early years will fundamentally change your kids' lives.

KNOWLEDGE (Life Skill)—See Lesson 16
Knowledge is achieved through dedication and hard work but the rewards are immense as it is *awesome power.* Application and transfer of knowledge to daily living is all important.

L

LEADERSHIP (Life Skill)—See Lesson 19
Parents have the responsibility of "showing the way" for their children. Leadership skills are teachable and kids need to learn these skills in the home. *Lead with integrity.*

LEARNING OUTCOMES—See Chapter Three
Practice, practice, practice makes the character difference! The central desired learning outcome is the development of good character in children exhibited by practiced values.

LIFE FOOTPRINTS (Activity)—See Lesson 1
The footprints that kids leave on the "sands of time" can be greatly enhanced by parents working to fully develop the skills and talents of their children. The potential of us all is unlimited!

MOTIVATION (Life Skill)—See Lesson 3
Parents need to teach their kids about how combining *enthusiasm* with *passion* produces great motivation. Kids need to know that "being bored" is an insult to their intelligence.

N

NEVER, NEVER, NEVER GIVE UP!—See Lesson 4
The hallmark of the Championship Family is the principle of never giving up. No family is perfect and everyone of them must hang in to overcome adversity and beat the odds.

NO EXCUSES (Activity)—See Lesson 17
One of life's best strategies is to follow the "no excuse" option. Kids need to learn how this option focuses emphasis on them taking sole responsibility for their actions and consequences.

O

ORGANIZATION (Life Skill)—See Lesson 20
A Championship Family has to take charge of its time and possessions to be free to live and have fun. Disorganization is a burden that has to be shed. *Organize for success!*

P

PARENTS—See MESSAGE to PARENTS
Parenting is without doubt one tough and demanding job. Following the CHARACTER PARENTING GAME PLAN offers a parenting blueprint that is value driven for success.

PARENTS AS COACHES AND TEACHERS—
See CHAMPIONSHIP FAMILY
Parents must actively coach and teach their kids through the lessons, activities, and journal work included in this book. Parents must be ready and willing to spend quality time with their kids.

PERSEVERANCE (Life Skill)—See Lesson 4
To persist is to unleash a powerful force that can accomplish seemingly impossible tasks. All family members need to realize the power of just trying one more time!

PRACTICE SESSIONS (Learning Outcomes)—See Chapter Three
Intended learning outcomes include: COMMUNICATION, CONFIDENCE, JUDGMENT, KNOWLEDGE, and RESPONSIBILITY. Practicing these values will last a lifetime.

PROFILE IN COURAGE (Activity)—See Lesson 11
Kids learn that a true hero is someone who has bravely displayed their commitment to values despite the cost or sacrifice. Anyone can be a hero anyplace at anytime.

PURSUE (Life Satisfaction)—See Chapter Five: SOAR to THRIVE
Parents need to connect their kids to the mindset of "STRIVING TO ACHIEVE OR ACCOMPLISH, ADVANCING RELENTLESSLY." This is an important part of life satisfaction.

R

READING—See Lesson 16
Parents, as their child's first teacher, have the primary responsibility of ensuring that their children have basic reading skills. If a student in school cannot read, the parents have failed them.

RESPECT (Core Value)—See Lesson 5
Once children learn that *thinking of others first* is vital, the concept of what respect is can fall into place. No child should ever go to school without the value of respect firmly established.

RESPONSIBILITY (Core Value)—See Lesson 17
There is no one else responsible for the health and welfare of a family but the parent. A parents' unwavering commitment to their families is mandatory otherwise the enterprise will fail.

RESUME (Activity)—See Lesson 14
Children who can list their short and long term goals along with the values that they practice, will in the future produce awesome job resumes. *Great lives are started early with values.*

S

SERVICE (Core Value)—See Lesson 21
Families who have learned that serving is the greatest reward have

gained a large share of a "Championship Season." Giving to others is getting a lot more back in return.

SERVICE ABOVE SELF (Activity)—See Lesson 21
It is important for families to engage in different community service activities together! Kids need to experience how they are connected to the community and how they can help.

SEVEN STEPS (Activity)—See Lesson 18
Kids need experience in problem solving and learn how procrastination can be overcome. Being a self-starter is all important as that one quality is critical to getting jobs done.

SHOOTING STARS (Activity)—See Lesson 3
First, parents work to motivate their children; then kids learn how to motivate themselves in completing tasks and starting new ones. *Become a motivated and enthusiastic person!*

SOAR (Life Satisfaction)—See Chapter Five: SOAR to THRIVE
Parents need to connect their kids to the mindset of "CLIMBING SWIFTLY, RISING ABOVE THE ORDINARY." This is an important part of life satisfaction.

T

TACT (Core Value)—See Lesson 22
Upholding the values and the integrity of people thereby unfolding understanding is not only needed in families but throughout today's very troubled and at-risk world.

TEAMWORK (Life Skill)—See Lesson 23
Being together does not ensure teamwork, a game plan is needed and that is what the CHARACTER PARENTING GAME PLAN is all about. Take the time for group hugs!

THRIVE (Life Satisfaction)—See Chapter Five: SOAR to THRIVE
Parents need to connect their kids to the mindset of "FLOURISHING WITH PURPOSE AND ENERGY, SELF-ACTUALIZING." This is an important part of life satisfaction.

TRAINING CAMP (Basics)—See Chapter One
Parents have to literally take their children to a "training camp" to learn about values and how to apply them to daily living. Values just don't happen, they must be learned over time.

TRUTH (Core Value)—See Lesson 12
Parents need to buy into the thought that *character parenting is truthful parenting*. Honesty and integrity are mandatory in the Championship Family; no exceptions to honoring the truth.

U

UNITY—See Lesson 23
The family must be a unified and united team of people to become a Championship Family. Unity is born out of having a common ground of Core and Life Skill values.

V

VIRTUE (Core Value)—See Lesson 24
Virtue is not a final destination but a summit we are trying to scale throughout life. Virtue is a capstone value that families need to be mindful of and in its daily pursuit.

VISION
Parents must pledge and dedicate themselves to become the character coaches for their children. Parents must give their children the priceless gift of great values!

W

WORK IN PROGRESS—See FAMILY JOURNAL
The Family Journal will reveal a family moving forward. Growing and learning never cease in our lives but we must be committed to making satisfactory progress in our endeavors.

WOW!—See CHAMPIONSHIP FAMILY-CHARACTER PARENTING Book
The potential of this book is boundless. Ideas have both power and wings. Once engaged, the outcomes of value driven lives is truly inspirational and to "infinity and beyond."

X

EXTRA-SPECIAL—See Lesson 10
If parents could do just one thing, it would be to make their kids and themselves feel extra-special because they are! Never be afraid to show your love for your family, they deserve it!

Y

YEARBOOK—See FAMILY JOURNAL
Every January, the family should think about publishing a yearbook highlighting the past year's contributions to the Family Journal. Time is well spent reflecting on a past family year.

Z

ZAP—See THRIVE
A great lesson learned is how to thrive throughout your years. The answer is to strike forcefully with your ready arsenal of Core and Life Skill values unleashing immense firepower!

ZIG & ZAG—See PURSUE
Following through is many times very difficult. The answer is to be able to execute a series of sharp turns or reversals as needed. Values give you this resiliency and adaptability.

ZIP—See IMAGINE
Using the power of imagination can be frustrating until you shift your mind into high gear to proceed swiftly and energetically to consider new ideas and ways to apply your values.

ZING—See CREATE
The creation process is really never easy which is why putting a little "vivacious and lively" energy into the task will help get you going. Values keep you energized and on target!

ZOOM—See SOAR
To let yourself climb swiftly means that you must let your engines go full throttle as you hear the resulting buzz or hum! Values will add to the *zooming* noise you make!

❖❖❖

My hope is that this book has put a little ZAP, ZIG *&* ZAG, ZIP, ZING *and* ZOOM *into the life of your family and into your character values.*

—GD

Works Cited

Bennett, William J., Chester E. Erin and John T.E. Cribb. *The Educated Child*. New York, NY: The Free Press/Simon & Schuster, 1999.

Bickel, Bruce, and Jantz, Stan. *Real Life is a Contact Sport*. Ann Arbor, MI: Vine Books/ Servant, 2000.

Clark, Ron. *The Essential 55*. New York, NY: Hyperion, 2003.

Covey, Stephen R. *The 7 Habits of Highly Effective People*. New York, NY. Fireside/Simon & Schuster, 1990.

Dobson, James C. *Parenting Isn't for Cowards*. Waco, TX: Word Books, 1987.

Fedorschak, Karuna. *Parenting*. New York, NY: MJF Books/Fine Communications, 2003.

Gorn, Elliot J, ed. *The McGuffey Readers—Selections from the 1879 Edition*. Boston, MA: Bedford/St. Martin's Press, 1998.

Gruwell, Erin. *The Freedom Writers Diary*. New York, NY: Broadway Books, 1999.

Levine, Karen. *Keeping Life Simple*. New York, NY: Barnes and Noble/Storey Communications, 1996.

Lickona, Thomas. *Educating for Character*. New York, NY: Bantam Books, 1992.

Maxwell, John C. *Attitude 101*. Nashville, TN: Thomas Nelson Publishers, 2003.

______. *The Power of Leadership*. Tulsa, OK. River Oak Publishing, 2001.

McGraw, Phil. *Family First*. New York, NY: Free Press/Simon and Schuster, 2004.

McGuffey's Eclectic Primer. New York, NY: Henry H. Vail, 1909. John

Wiley and Sons, Inc.
McGuffey's First Eclectic Reader. New York, NY: Henry H. Vail, 1920. John Wiley and Sons, Inc.

McGuffey's Second Eclectic Reader. New York, NY: Henry H. Vail, 1920. John Wiley and Sons, Inc.

McGuffey's Third Eclectic Reader. New York, NY: Henry H. Vail, 1920. John Wiley and Sons, Inc.

McGuffey's Fourth Eclectic Reader. New York, NY: Henry H. Vail, 1920. John Wiley and Sons, Inc.

McGuffey's Fifth Eclectic Reader. New York, NY: Henry H. Vail, 1920. John Wiley and Sons, Inc.

McGuffey's Sixth Eclectic Reader. New York, NY: Henry H. Vail, 1921. John Wiley and Sons, Inc.

NIV Quest Study Bible. Grand Rapids, MI: Zondervan, 2003.

Salwak, Dale. *Faith in the Family*. Novato, CA: New World Library, 2001.

Stepanek, Mattie J.T. *Heartsongs*. New York, NY: Hyperion, 2001.

Stewart, Marjabelle Young. *Little Ways to Say You Care*. New York, NY: MJF Books/Fine Communications, 1992.

Wilson, James Q. *The Moral Sense*. New York, NY: Free Press/Simon and Schuster, 1993.

Wooden, John, and Steve Jamison. *Wooden*. Chicago, IL: Contemporary Books, 1997.

Wright, Susan. *Clutter Control*. New York, NY: Barnes and Noble/Carol Publishing Group, 1991.